An All-Access Tour Through

BOTH TESTAMENTS

BACKSTAGE PASS

to the Bible

Leader's Guide

Backstage Pass to the Bible: Leader's Guide

Copyright © 2002 by CWR Production, P.O. Box 230, Farnham, Surrey, GU9 8XG, England.

Youth Specialties Books, 300 S. Pierce St., El Cajon, CA 92020, are published by Zondervan Publishing House, 5300 Patterson Ave. S.E., Grand Rapids, MI 49530.

Library of Congress Cataloging-in-Publication Data

Brant, Jonathan, 1970-
    Backstage Pass the Bible : leader's guide / Jonathan Brant.
      p. cm.
    "Youth Specialties."
    ISBN 0-310-24926-0 (pbk. : alk. paper)
    1. Bible—Study and teaching. 2. Christian education of young people.
I. Title.
BS600.2 .B723 2000
20.6'1'071—dc21

                                           99-053045

Edited by Andrew Wooding, Vicki Newby, Tim McLaughlin, Linnea Lagerquist and Rick Marschall
Production Assistance by Sarah Sheerin and Nicole Davis
Cover and interior design by David Folkman/Larry Brown Graphic Design
Illustrated by David Yapp
Additional research and concepts contributed by Tricia Brant and Jim Hancock
Formally published as Downloading the Bible: Leader's Guide

Printed in the United States of America

02 03 04 05 06 07 08 / ML / 10 9 8 7 6 5 4 3 2 1

An All-Access Tour Through
BOTH TESTAMENTS

BACKSTAGE PASS
to the Bible

Jonathan **Brant**

CWR

ys
Youth Specialties

ZONDERVAN™
WWW.ZONDERVAN.COM

Leader's Guide

Contents

Session 1   Backstage Pass to the Bible   6

Session 2   The Historical Books of the Old Testament   14

Session 3   The Books of Poetry and Wisdom   24

Session 4   The Old Testament Prophets   33

Session 5   The Gospels   42

Session 6   The Books of Acts   52

Session 7   The New Testament Letters   59

Session 8   The Book of Revelation   65

Divide into small groups creatively!   75

Backstage Pass to the Bible

Use a video clip or a game for

Opening Act

Armageddon the movie

Bruce Willis, Ben Affleck, Liv Tyler

Start 2:02 NASA control center, after a spiraling camera shot out of drill hole
Stop 2:06 Lift goes back up into shuttle, leaving Harry (Bruce Willis) alone on asteroid. He says, "This was a really good idea!"

If you've been a youth leader for even a year, you've been driven to the brink of insanity more than your share of times by technology that refuses to work when you need it. What's worse, while you're bent over the malfunctioning and malevolent equipment, doing your darndest not to cuss at it, your students are going ballistic, yelling, offering less than helpful advice, and generally adding insult to injury.

So here's a not-to-be-missed opportunity to turn the tables on them—your chance to drive *them* to the brink of insanity for a change! As you show this clip from *Armageddon*, perform some insidious acts with the remote from where you sit: change the channel just as things get exciting ... lower the sound at moments of critical dialogue ... foul the tracking just when they need to see exactly what's happening on the screen. You get the idea. And to inflict the maximum misery, try to conceal your video sabatoge, at least the first minute or two of the clip.

After the film clip make these introductory points—

▶ **Frustrating to watch, huh? Just goes to show that, if you mess with a movie's sound and the video enough—if you can't see or hear what's going on—it's impossible to really follow and understand the story.**

▶ **Let's face it—reading the Bible can sometimes be just as frustrating. There are times when**

everything is clear and simple and meaningful, but there are also times when it seems like the tracking is shot, the sound fades in and out-and in the space of a few verses, you're not sure if you're watching the cynical violence of *Pulp Fiction* or the impossible sweetness of *Mary Poppins*. When the Bible gets confusing, it quickly becomes complicated, frustrating, and boring.

▶ **Today we're starting some sessions that will make the Bible a bit easier to understand and will lessen your confusion or frustration with it.**

Reverse Pictionary
the game
What you'll need
- ☑ Whiteboard and markers
- ☑ One drawing pen per group
- ☑ A list of objects for players to draw (leaf, book, car, coffee mug, cell phone, broccoli, etc.)

In a phrase, Reverse Pictionary is the regular Pictionary turned upside down and inside out. Here's the quirk: the students with pens in their hands and white expanses in front of them don't have a clue what they're supposed to be drawing. In fact, they're the ones who have to guess!

Don't panic—this is not a curriculum on ESP and other mystical phenomena.

Before you begin, and if you have more than 20 in your group, divide your kids into two teams and compete team against team (see **Divide into Small Groups Creatively!** on page 75). If there are less than 20 kids in your group, you can quite happily all stay together—the more people, the greater the confusion, and the better it'll be!

> Throughout this book, white board and markers are listed for activities that require writing for the entire group's viewing. Of course you can also use an overhead projector, a flip chart, or butcher paper taped on the wall, depending on your setting and available resources.

Choose the first artist, then ask her to leave the room or cover her eyes while the word is revealed to the rest of the group. Then ask the artist to take up her pen and draw while the rest of the group instructs her how to draw the object–without describing any part of the object. For instance, team members cannot say, "Draw a wheel!" or "Draw a screen!"–they are allowed only terms like *straight line, curve, circle, rectangle, horizontal, vertical,* and *square.*

Start with simple objects (leaf, book, car) and progress to more complex objects (coffee mug, cell phone, broccoli). Add a time limit if your group is doing well. You'll be amazed at how hard it is to instruct someone in how to draw a recognizable representation of even the simplest object–and with every member of the group shouting instructions to the artist, you are likely to see some very strange pictures!

At the end of each attempt, let the artist guess the object from her own rendering of it. Then write the name of the object under the drawing–whether or not the artist was ever able to decipher it!

After 10 minutes or so of the game, make the transition to the lesson with words along this line (and if you still have some of the less successful drawings, show them to the group as you talk).

▶ Didn't you just want to scream when the artist couldn't follow your perfectly precise and simple instructions? But then when *you* were the artist, it wasn't your fault at all–it was everyone yelling vague instructions at you! Under the duress of the moment, you concluded that they have more fingers than brain cells and couldn't give clear, helpful instructions on how to replace a light bulb.

▶ As a general rule, it's frustrating when something we assumed was simple becomes difficult and confusing.

▶ You may feel similarly now and then when reading the Bible. There are times when everything is clear and simple and meaningful, but there are also times when the Bible seems harder to decipher than some of the drawings we saw during the game. The Bible just becomes complicated, frustrating, and boring.

▶ Today we're starting some sessions that will make the Bible a bit easier to understand and will lessen your confusion or frustration with it.

Let the Show Begin!

What you'll need
☑ Photocopies of the Staging Sheet **A READING IN LUKE** (page 11)
☑ Four students who have rehearsed this reading at least once

After the students complete the dramatic reading, say something like this–

▶ The only Bible Jesus and his followers had was the Hebrew Bible–what Christians now call the Old Testament. And no, the Hebrew Bible didn't have a cross on its cover. In fact, it didn't have a cover, because it was a scroll. A big scroll, too–too big to carry around under your arm.

▶ The point is, it's easy for us to miss what it was Jesus was talking about when he talked about "the Scripture"–we tend to picture *nice little portable book*, not *big fat scroll the size of a sleeping bag.*

▶ In a similar way, these two disciples of Jesus had clearly missed the point in a big way. And even when the Man himself was *walking right next to them*–the Word itself–not even then did they get it. Until the moment he left them, that is.

▶ We may not have the Man himself walking right next to us–literally, that is–but we do have God's Holy Spirit to help us. And we have intelligence and experience and insight that God has given each of us, of course.

▶ If we learn a little about the Bible . . . about the different books and styles of writing . . . about the historical events and places that it talks about–then the Bible can become much less confusing and frustrating to read.

Check Out the Lyrics
and put them to work

For middle schoolers
Map It!

What you'll need
- ☑ Familiarity with the info on pages 18-21 of Backstage OT or NT
- ☑ A whiteboard and markers
- ☑ Copies of the Staging Sheet MAP IT! (page 12)
- ☑ Pens and Bibles

Be prepared to present the information from pages 18-21 of *Backstage OT* or *NT*. Start out with something like this—

▶ **Many people are totally convinced that the Bible is God's Word. Other people—just as nice, just as intelligent—are absolutely sure that it's just a big, old book to use for propping doors open or pressing flowers.**

Invite your students to call out—
1. Reasons some people believe that the Bible is God's Word
2. Reasons other people believe that the Bible is nothing particularly special

On the board, write down their two lists of ideas. Then say something like—

▶ **With something as important as the Bible, we should expect such debate over it. Yet there's plenty of evidence—even proof—why it should be considered more than just a big, old book.**

▶ **The Bible was written by many different human authors. They all had different personalities, styles, interests-differences that show themselves in the books they wrote. But they were all inspired by God and led by him to write what they did-God's Word.**

▶ **Want proof? Check out the incredible unity of thought on all the key issues. Consider the amazing impact the Bible has had—and continues to have—on the lives of millions of people living all around the world.**

Pair up your students, hand out the Staging Sheet **Map It!** (page 12), and give 'em five or 10 minutes to work. Your crowd might need help keeping straight the different styles of writing on the table, so be ready to explain *biography, history, proverbs, prophecy, poetry, song,* and *letters.* When time's up, call all the pairs back together to compare how everybody filled in the handout.

Then read aloud this help-wanted ad.

> ### W a n t e d
> Man or woman to write Holy Scripture. Start immediately, pay and benefits negotiable.
> Send resume to
> Angel in Charge
> Perfect Personnel Dept.
> Bldg. 777, Holy Highway
> Jerusalem City, Heaven

Now ask the group to brainstorm questions like these—

▶ **What qualifications would you expect the successful applicant to have?**

▶ **What kind of background and experience would be helpful?**

just when I was getting to the good part

moses

 tea time!

wifey

Since *Backstage Pass to the Bible: An All-Access Tour Through the Old Testament* and *Backstage Pass to the Bible: An All-Access Tour Through the New Testament* are way too long for you to read every time, this Leader's Guide uses a shorthand title for each: *Backstage OT* and *Backstage NT*. Since you're so smart, you'll know what it means.

Write all the ideas, even the loopy ones, onto a whiteboard. Once you've restored some order, make this point—

▶ **God used all types of people to write the Bible.**

▶ **Some were highly educated or highly religious; these would have known how to write a hot resume. Others were simple working people, farmers and fishermen—not the sort of people you'd pay to write your English assignment for you, let alone the Bible.**

For high schoolers (Greatest hits)
What's Behind the Music?

What you'll need
☑ Copies of the Staging Sheet
What's Behind the Music? (page 13)
☑ Whiteboard and markers
☑ Pens and Bibles

Divide the students into work groups of four or five (see **Divide into Small Groups Creatively!** on page 75), and hand out copies of the Staging Sheet **What's Behind the Music?** (page 13). Each group should have access to at least one Bible. Say something like—

▶ *God's Word.* **You've heard the Bible called this maybe a thousand times. Let's explore what it means-and look at some of the reasons why so many people believe it's true. Let's start by doing the first part of the Staging Sheet you're holding, "Who's the true author of the Bible?"**

While they're working individually or in small groups for five or 10 minutes, you draw on the whiteboard the same graph they're working on. When you regather the group, plot on the graph the responses of the kids or the small groups–then find the average for the whole group or have your students do it. You should end up with a number somewhere in the middle of the graph.

Which is just what one would expect! Explain why—

▶ **While we firmly believe-and the Bible explicitly states-that God is the true author of the Bible, it was not written by some kind of divine dictation or spiritual shorthand. Yes, God inspired the writers by his Holy Spirit, but in unique ways that took into account the writers' different personalities, situations, and cultures. And if you look for it, you can see the writers' individualism and humanity come across in the books of the Bible.**

If time allows, discuss the last two questions on their Staging Sheet. Then sum up with words to this effect–

▶ **Consider The Big Questions: What is the origin of the Universe? Does God exist? Is humanity basically good or evil? What happens when you die?**

In the Wings
Little and often . . . and time traveling

Some of your students–and for some youth groups, *most* students—will come to these Bible sessions with a bunch of negative experiences that will color their thinking and their expectations. Here's their chance to lay aside all that and start their relationship with the Bible afresh. The first approach to Bible reading is called Little and Often (*Backstage OT or NT*, page 13). Explain—

▶ **No matter how many times you fail, no matter how many times you forget your elaborate plans, no matter how many times you drift back to sleep when you swore you'd be reading the Bible-all that matters is that you just keep going. Keep dipping in, open the Bible again and** again, start afresh as many times as you have to. Do anything-just don't stop reading the Bible!

The second is the Time Travelers' Way (*Backstage OT or NT*, page 13). Tell your group—

As you read the Bible, ask yourself–

▶ **What this passage meant to those who first read it in the *past*?**

▶ **What does this passage means to you right now in your life in the *present*?**

▶ **What are you are going to do or think differently in the *future* as a result of what this passage says?**

▶ The Big Questions are hard ones that usually create disagreement if not an all-out argument—even among friends. Taylor's a dreamer—thinks we're descended from alien spacemen, the ones who really built the pyramids. Amy's a softie—she thinks humans must be basically good because her baby niece is just so sweet (at least when her diaper's not full). Franny's a scientist—she knows the truth, we've all evolved from animals . . . in fact, she's downright proud to have an orangutang in her family tree.

▶ Yet when it comes to The Big Questions (and a lot of other issues, too), all the authors of the Bible are in perfect agreement! This unusual agreement is at least a little evidence that the Bible is more than just a normal book!

▶ No other book continues to have such a profound effect on the people who read it.

Take a Bow

Conclude with this, based on pages 16–17 of *Backstage OT*.

▶ Our God is a creative genius. The proof is in the world that surrounds us—the world he created. Think of all the different tastes and smells. Think of all the bizarre animals, like platypuses or naked mole rats. What about different landscapes, from tropical jungles to blistering deserts? And just compare Arnold Schwarzenegger with Cindy Crawford. The world is full of the weird and the wonderful!

▶ The Bible is chock-full of the epic, the exciting, the mysterious, the bizarre—and it's the incredibly creative and exciting way that God has chosen to make himself known. In fact, it's just the kind of introduction we would expect from a creative genius.

▶ Just like anything else, to get the most out of the Bible we must make some effort of our own. If you want to excel at photography, fencing, Foosball, or finger-picking the guitar, you've gotta practice—and it's the same with the Bible. If you want to understand and learn from it, you've gotta be willing to think a little.

Staging Sheet

A Reading in Luke

Luke 24:13-33

MS & HS

Characters

Narrator

Jesus

Cleopas, a disciple of Jesus

A second disciple

Although this is pretty much straight from the Bible, it should be read dramatically.

NARRATOR: Now that same day two of them were going to a village called Emmaus, about seven miles from Jerusalem. They were talking with each other about everything that had happened. As they talked and discussed these things with each other, Jesus himself came up and walked along with them; but they were kept from recognizing him.

JESUS: What are you discussing together as you walk along?

NARRATOR: They stood still, their faces downcast. One of them, named Cleopas, asked him—

CLEOPAS: Are you only a visitor to Jerusalem and do not know the things that have happened there in these days?

JESUS: What things?

SECOND DISCIPLE: About Jesus of Nazareth. He was a prophet, powerful in word and deed before God and all the people. The chief priests and our rulers handed him over to be sentenced to death, and they crucified him; but we had hoped that he was the one who was going to redeem Israel. And what is more, it is the third day since all this took place. In addition, some of our women amazed us. They went to the tomb early this morning but didn't find his body.

They came and told us that they had seen a vision of angels, who said he was alive. Then some of our companions went to the tomb and found it just as the women had said, but him they did not see.

JESUS: How foolish you are, and how slow of heart to believe all that the prophets have spoken! Did not the Christ have to suffer these things and then enter his glory?

NARRATOR: And beginning with Moses and all the Prophets, he explained to them what was said in all the Scriptures concerning himself. As they approached the village to which they were going, Jesus acted as if he were going farther. But they urged him to stay.

CLEOPAS: Stay with us, for it is nearly evening; the day is almost over.

NARRATOR: So he went in to stay with them. When he was at the table with them, he took bread, gave thanks, broke it and began to give it to them. Then their eyes were opened and they recognized him, and he disappeared from their sight.

CLEOPAS: Were not our hearts burning within us while he talked with us on the road and opened the Scriptures to us?

NARRATOR: They got up and returned at once to Jerusalem.

END

A map is one way to help us keep track of what's happening in the Bible. And there are lots of ways to map the Bible—one of which is to map its parts. Use your Bible to help you fill in the blanks.

MS

OLD TESTAMENT

Five Books   Genesis, Exodus, Leviticus, _____, Deuteronomy

Historical Books   Joshua, _____, Ruth, 1 Samuel, 2 Samuel, 1 Kings, 2 Kings, 1 Chronicles, 2 Chronicles, Ezra, Nehemiah, Esther

Poetry and Wisdom   Job, _____, Proverbs, Ecclesiastes, Song of Songs

The Prophets   Isaiah, Jeremiah, Lamentations, Ezekiel, Daniel, Hosea, Joel, Amos, Obadiah, _____, Micah, Nahum, Habakkuk, Zephaniah, Haggai, Zechariah, Malachi

NEW TESTAMENT

The Gospels   Matthew, Mark, _____, John

Acts   The Acts of the Apostles (Acts)

Paul's Letters   Romans, 1 Corinthians, 2 Corinthians, _____, Ephesians, Philippians, Colossians, 1 Thessalonians, 2 Thessalonians, _____, _____, Titus, Philemon

Other Letters   Hebrews, _____, 1 Peter, 2 Peter, 1 John, 2 John, 3 John, Jude

Revelation   Revelation

Another way to map the Bible is by the different kinds of writing it contains. This table lists the seven main ones. Your job? Put each of the books in the column where it belongs. Here are some hints: Luke goes under biography, Psalms goes under song, Titus goes under letters . . . and can you guess where Proverbs goes?

BIOGRAPHY	HISTORY	PROVERBS	POETRY	SONG	PROPHECY	LETTERS

What's Behind the Music?

Who's the true author of the Bible, God or humans? Well, what does the Bible say? Look up each of the Bible references below. Plot each verse, on the graph according to how strongly you think it supports God's authorship or humans-authorship. The first one, 2 Timothy 3:16, has been done for you.

MS

The value for 2 Timothy 3:16 is 2. Add up the values of the five references and divide by five to get your average.

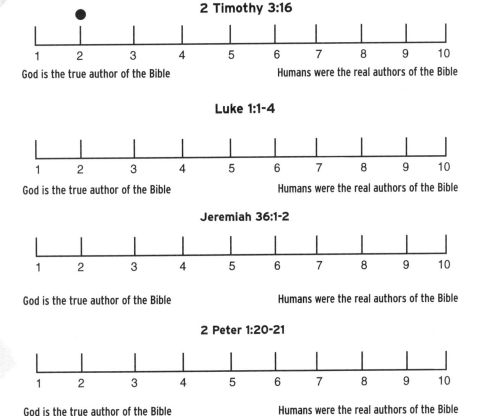

2 Timothy 3:16

| 1 | 2 | 3 | 4 | 5 | 6 | 7 | 8 | 9 | 10 |

God is the true author of the Bible   Humans were the real authors of the Bible

Luke 1:1-4

| 1 | 2 | 3 | 4 | 5 | 6 | 7 | 8 | 9 | 10 |

God is the true author of the Bible   Humans were the real authors of the Bible

Jeremiah 36:1-2

| 1 | 2 | 3 | 4 | 5 | 6 | 7 | 8 | 9 | 10 |

God is the true author of the Bible   Humans were the real authors of the Bible

2 Peter 1:20-21

| 1 | 2 | 3 | 4 | 5 | 6 | 7 | 8 | 9 | 10 |

God is the true author of the Bible   Humans were the real authors of the Bible

1 Corinthians 16:19-21

| 1 | 2 | 3 | 4 | 5 | 6 | 7 | 8 | 9 | 10 |

God is the true author of the Bible   Humans were the real authors of the Bible

NOW DISCUSS THESE TWO QUESTIONS

▶ If God is the true author of the book we call the Bible, how would we expect the Bible to differ from any other collection of 67 books written as much as centuries apart and by a widely differing group of authors?

▶ If the Bible is more than just a book, we would expect people to be deeply affected by it and to respond to it differently than to any other book. Have you yourselves experienced anything unique about the Bible? Or do you know of other people who have been strongly affected by it? If so, how have you—or they—been affected?

The Historical Books of the Old Testament

Use a video clip or a game for

Opening Act

Groundhog Day the movie

Bill Murray

Start 0:55 Alarm clock fills the screen as it flicks over yet again to 6:00 a.m. Phil (Bill Murray) lies in bed in his pajamas, already depressed
Stop 1:01 After his suicide attempt, Phil is awakened once again by his alarm clock. He says, "Oh, nuts!"

Introduce the clip like this—

▶ **Remember *Groundhog Day*? About the self-centered and arrogant TV weatherman who finds himself trapped in a small town, repeating the worst day of his life over and over and over again? As you'll see here, no matter what he does, his alarm wakes him up each morning at six a.m. in the same bed in the same hotel as if the previous day had never even happened.**

. . . and end it with something like—

▶ **If you didn't know what a *vicious circle* was before, you do now.**

Caterpillar Races
the game
What you'll need

- ☑ **Groups of five to eight students**
- ☑ **A straight racecourse about 15 feet long**
- ☑ **A circular race track marked with tape or chairs**

A youth group can be like a screaming baby. No matter how much you love your students, aren't there times when you'd be willing to go to any lengths (well, *almost* any lengths) just to get them to calm down and be quiet for a few minutes? If you know this feeling, this game's for you.

This one is so physically demanding that the Marines probably use it in boot camp. In any case, it's a guaranteed group quieter.

First, you need caterpillars. Caterpillars are made of kids, five to eight of 'em.

The five to eight students sit down one behind the other, all facing forward and scrunched up as close together as possible. Once they're arranged, they put their hands on the shoulders of the person in front of them, and their legs around that person's waist so that their feet are resting in the lap of the person in front of them.

Once they have done this, they will find that the only part of their anatomy resting on the floor is their bottoms. (Depending on what you think of games requiring physical contact, you may want to make the caterpillars just-guy, just-girl, or mixed.) For the caterpillar to move, its teenage segments must waddle on its five to eight buttocks.

It's not easy, either! It requires coordination and hard work to get anywhere. Now for the races.

▶ **Xtreme Crawling.** A straightforward race of speed among *all* your group's caterpillars. Create a straight racecourse (no longer than 15 feet, unless you want blisters in unfortunate places) with a starting line and a finish line. The winner is the first caterpillar to cross the finish line without disintegrating or using their hands.

▶ **Catch Me If You Can.** Create a circular race-track in the middle of the floor. (Use masking tape, orange traffic cones, even a few chairs to mark the course.) Read on about the race itself, and then you'll have a better idea how long to make it. Position two caterpillars so that they face the same direction, but are starting on opposite sides of the circular track. On "Go!" they start waddling—and whichever caterpillar catches up and touches the back of the other wins. Ideally though not necessarily, the course should be long enough so that the racing caterpillars become exhausted *before* there is any clear winner—a standoff that will help you make a key point later in the session. Let all the little insects have a shot at this race.

Open the Bible and

Let the Show Begin!

What you'll need

☑ **Four Bibles or four copies of A READING IN JUDGES (page 19)**
☑ **Four students (selected before the start of the session) to read these verses**

This session looks at the vicious circle the Israelites got themselves into during the times of the Judges. You won't explain this to your group yet, but the posture of each reader corresponds to Israel's fortunes as reflected in the verse of Judges chapter 3 (page 19) read by that student—

READER 1 reads verse 7–
sitting or kneeling on the floor
READER 2 reads verse 8–
standing to the left of Student 1
READER 3 reads verses 9-10–
standing on a chair immediately behind Student 1
READER 4 reads verse 11–
standing to the right of Student 1
READER 1 reads verse 12

After the reading, say something like—

▶ **At first sight this appears to be a spectacularly uninspiring piece of ancient history. It makes you want to throw your hands in the air and scream, "So what?!" I mean, it teaches us nothing about God, it doesn't seem to have a decent moral . . . frankly, reading the backs of cornflake boxes is more interesting. So why is it in the Bible at all?**

▶ **Hang onto your seats while we try to answer that question. Also we'll–**

  ▷ **explore why there is so much history in the Bible**

  ▷ **find out what is going on in this particular case**

  ▷ **ask what it might mean to us today**

Check Out the Lyrics
and put them to work

For middle schoolers
It's just a phase

What you'll need

☑ **Copies of the Staging Sheet It's Just a Phase (middle school version, pages 20-21)**
☑ **One drawing pen per group**

Summarize the "Historical Books" section in Backstage Pass OT on pages 54-55. First you may want to—

▶ Get a handle on how the events recorded in the historical books fit into the flow of the Old Testament as a whole. See "Dancing Through the Old Testament" in Backstage Pass OT on pages 26-39.

▶ Take a quick look at the illustrations on the Staging Sheet **It's Just a Phase** (middle school version, pages 20-21) to make sure that you give enough information for your students to fill in the summaries.

Be sure you cover these key points.

▶ **The Old Testament books from Genesis to Nehemiah are *history books*. They tell the story of the nation of Israel from the time of creation all the way till Israel's return from exile–which was just 400 years or so before the birth of Christ! The short section we just read takes place around the middle of that story–and it's all about vicious circles.**

bedtime reading

What you say next depends on which activity you started this session with.

If you opened this session with the Groundhog Day *clip, say something like this—*

▶ **During the Opening Act section just now we saw something of the horror of being forever stuck in a circle, going round and round and round and** never getting anywhere. It would be terrible to be trapped repeating even a great day over and over again, and the film maker is absolutely right—to have to continually repeat one of the worst days of your life would make you completely suicidal.

If you opened this session with the caterpillar races, say something like this—

▶ During the Opening Act section just now we saw something of the horror of being forever stuck in a circle, going round and round and round and never getting anywhere. It was downright painful to go waddling around and around on your bottom chasing another caterpillar!

Now, whichever way you started this session, say this—

▶ Strangely, this is exactly how many religions see history—an endless and purposeless cycle of death and reincarnation in which your life never makes a difference. Yet what the history books of the Old Testament make clear is that history is not like that. Our God is always working toward a wonderful goal, and our lives have real purpose and meaning.

Hand out the copies of the Staging Sheet **It's Just a Phase** (middle school version, pages 20-21) and allow the students 10 minutes to work on them with a partner.

In the final few minutes of this section of the session, call the group back together and explain to them—

In the Wings
Vicious Circles

What you'll need

☑ Lengths of string or thick yarn, each long enough to tie into a circle, enough for all your students (it's best if you lay strings on each chair before the session begins)

☑ Scissors

During this session your students may have thought of vicious circles in their own lives. This is a symbolic exercise for kids who want to break out of such circles and cycles. The exercise asks them to take the string that was on their chair when they entered the room and tie the ends together in a knot—thus making a circle. Ask those who want to publicly demonstrate their desire to break out of their vicious circle to come forward, pair up with another brave soul, and then—with whatever words of prayer or ceremony you may want to lead them in—snip each other's string circle with scissors.

That's the ceremony. You can say something like this—

▶ Remember the vicious circle the Israelites were trapped in? I'm sorry to have to be the one to break it to you, but vicious circles are not merely ancient phenomena. They didn't die out with

the dinosaurs or disappear with the dodo. They still exist and are very much alive and kicking—and each of us can name at least a couple or three in our own lives.

▶ You're well aware of the range of vicious circles that you're plagued by—

As the leader, decide how specific you should be before you list your students' likely vicious circles—

▶ Ignoring your Bible, ignoring prayer, gossiping, stubborn fighting with parents, substance abuse, sexual behavior that you sense isn't healthy, eating disorders. This might be a good time to ask for God's help to help you break free

Explain now the symbolic string ceremony. Afterward you can close with words to this effect—

▶ It took a long time for God to break the Israelites out of their vicious circle, but he did it in the end. It may take some time, or it may take a moment—but God will always be faithful to you!

- The vicious circle you've been studying is one small part of a terrible cycle that the Israelites found themselves trapped in throughout the period of history covered by the book of Judges.

- Don't despair, though. God didn't leave them there to rot forever. At the right time he helped them to break out of the vicious circle and to progress to a new stage in their history—the times of the Kings.

For high schoolers (Greatest hits)

It's just a phase

What you'll need

- ☑ Copies of the Staging Sheet IT'S JUST A PHASE (high school version, pages 22-23)
- ☑ Students in groups of four or five
- ☑ A whiteboard and markers

Divide your students into small groups of four or five (see Divide into Small Groups Creatively! on page 75).

Unless you're very familiar with Old Testament history, you may want to get a handle on how the events recorded in the historical books fit into the flow of the Old Testament as a whole—if so, skim through "Dancing Through the Old Testament" in *Backstage Pass OT* on pages 26-39.

Before you hand out the Staging Sheet, make these points.

- The Old Testament books from Genesis to Nehemiah are history books. They tell the story of the nation of Israel from the time of creation all the way till Israel's return from exile—which was just 400 years or so before the birth of Christ! The short section we just read takes place around the middle of that story—and it's all about vicious circles.

Now distribute the Staging Sheet **It's Just a Phase** (high school version, pages 22-23) and give the students 10 minutes to work in their groups.

Once this time is over call them back together.

- What you have worked on is some-times called a "vicious circle"—a negative pattern that keeps on repeating itself. The Israelites found them-selves trapped in this particular vicious circle

throughout the period of their history covered by the book of Judges. God did eventually break them out of it, and they progressed to the next stage: the times of the Kings.

- A few minutes ago during the Opening Act section we saw something of the horror of being forever stuck in a circle, going around and around and around and never getting anywhere.

If you opened this session with the Groundhog Day *clip, say something like this—*

- It would be terrible to be trapped repeating even a great day over and over again and the film maker is absolutely right, to have to repeat one of the worst days of your life over and over would make you completely suicidal.

If you opened this session with the caterpillar races, say something like this—

- It was downright painful to go waddling around and around on your bottom chasing another caterpillar!

Now, whichever way you started this session, say this—

▶ **Strangely, this is exactly how many religions see history-an endless and purposeless cycle of death and reincarnation where your life will never make a difference. What the history books of the Old Testament make clear is that history is not like that. Our God is always working toward a wonderful goal and our lives have real purpose and meaning.**

Now ask kids to call out the words and phrases they wrote down in the second page of the Staging Sheet. You should hear things like *evil . . . eyes of the Lord . . . anger of the Lord . . . cried out to the Lord . . . Spirit of the Lord*, etc.

As these are called out, make a note of them on a whiteboard. Then invite groups to read aloud their one-sentence responses from their Staging Sheet. Highlight for your kids two points that you can count on hearing in their responses: a moral aspect (good and evil, etc.) and God's involvement in this history.

Take a Bow

Time to conclude! You can do it with words to this effect—

▶ **I know that some of you just love your history classes at school and are even now planning to gain extra credit by writing a paper on the Kings of Katmandu. I also know that others of you think you hate history and have been tempted to jump from third-floor windows or swallow an entire package of laxatives just to have an excuse to escape class.**

▶ **However you feel about it, the fact is that the Bible is absolutely chock-full of history. And it's *real* history. Just because it appears in what is con-sidered a holy book doesn't mean that the writers had jelly for brains or couldn't be trusted to tell the truth. They were good historians. No archaeological find has ever disproved the history of the Old Testament. The history books of the Old Testament are more than just dry records of past events! They're intended to teach us about God and about his ways. That's why they're valuable to us, even thousands of years later.**

▶ **Some of these history books are given a special title-*prophetic history*, despite the apparent contradiction of those words. In fact, here's a little something for those of you who need to impress your English teacher: oxymoron. An oxymoron is a phrase composed of two seemingly contradictory words. *Thunderous silence, bittersweet, military intelligence, attractive youth leader, prophetic history* . . . get it? Actually, these books of prophetic history really aren't that contradictory. They teach about God and his action in the world (that's the prophetic part) through records of past events (that's the history part).**

A Reading in Judges

Staging Sheet   **Judges 3:7-12**

Characters

Reader 1 (sitting or kneeling on the floor)

Reader 2 (standing to the left of Reader 1)

Reader 3 (standing on a chair immediately behind Reader 1)

Reader 4 (standing to the right of Reader 1)

Although this is straight from the Bible, it should be read dramatically.

READER 1 The Israelites did evil in the eyes of the Lord; they forgot the Lord their God and served the Baals (BAY-uhls) and the Asherahs (Uh-SHEAR-uhs).

READER 2 The anger of the Lord burned against Israel so that he sold them into the hands of Cushan-Rishathaim (KOOSH-an rish-uh-THAY-im) king of Aram Naharaim (AIR-rum nay-huh-RAY-im), to whom the Israelites were subject for eight years.

READER 3 But when they cried out to the Lord, he raised up for them a deliverer, Othniel (OTH-nee-uhl) son of Kenaz (KEE-naz), Caleb's younger brother, who saved them. The Spirit of the Lord came upon him, so that he became Israel's judge and went to war. The Lord gave Cushan-Rishathaim (KOOSH-an rish-uh-THAY-im) king of Aram (AIR-rum) into the hands of Othniel (OTH-nee-uhl), who overpowered him.

READER 4 So the land had peace for forty years, until Othniel (OTH-nee-uhl) son of Kenaz (KEE-naz) died.

READER 1 Once again the Israelites did evil in the eyes of the Lord, and because they did this evil the Lord gave Eglon (EGG-lawn) king of Moab (MOE-ab) power over Israel.

END

it's just a phase

Part 1

MS

THE BIBLE SHOWS God working in history. Here are some stages in the history of the children of Israel. Look up these references in your Bible. Under each picture, write the correct Bible reference and a sentence that describes what's going on.

References: Genesis 1, 2; Genesis 6-8; Genesis 21-22; Exodus 12:28-34; Exodus 16-17; Joshua 10; Judges 2:16-23.

_____

_____

_____

_____

_____

_____

_____

_____

_____

_____

_____

_____

where we going?

_____

_____

_____

_____

_____

_____

_____

_____

_____

it's just a phase
Staging Sheet
Part 2

MS

IF TWO PEOPLE FIGHT and neither wants to work things out, the fight can get worse and worse. When that happens, what you've got is a vicious cycle. Well, the Israelites were stubborn that way too. Read Judges 3:7-12 to find out how. Then complete this vicious circle by writing a sentence about what's happening in each of the pictures.

_____
_____
_____

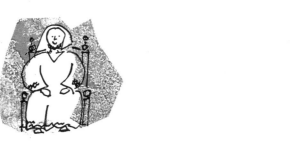

_____
_____
_____

_____
_____
_____

_____
_____
_____

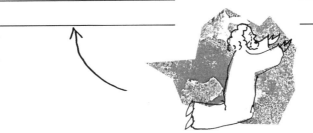

JUDGES 3:7-12 IS JUST PART of the ol' *dumb choices* ⇨ *repentance* ⇨ *more dumb choices* ⇨ *more repentance* cycle. The Israelites start off doing evil in the eyes of the Lord in verse 7, and by the time they arrive at verse 12, they're back at it again.

Read Judges 3:7–12 to find out how. Then complete this vicious circle by writing a sentence about what's happening in each of the pictures.

_____

_____

_____

_____

_____

_____

_____

_____

_____

_____

_____

_____

it's just a phase

Part 2

HS

THE LANGUAGE OF THE BOOK of Judges isn't your typical history textbook language. When you read the passage you'll probably notice a number of words and phrases that you wouldn't expect to see in the history books that you use at school. Write as many of these as you can find in the space below.

_____

_____

_____

_____

_____

_____

_____

_____

_____

_____

_____

Think about the history books you use at school. What's different about the way this passage writes about historical events? What's different about the words and phrases it uses? Write a one-sentence answer below and be prepared to share it with the group.

_____

_____

_____

_____

_____

_____

_____

_____

_____

_____

_____

_____

Session 3
The Books of Poetry and Wisdom

Use a video clip or a game for
Opening Act

Four Weddings and a Funeral the movie
Hugh Grant, Andie McDowell

Start 1:19 Scene change to rainy suburb at start of Gareth's funeral
Stop 1:24 The end of the funeral scene. During the funeral Gareth's best friend reads a poem to express the grief that he feels and can't put into words of his own

Poetry Recital
the game
What you'll need
- ☑ A poem, perhaps from Shel Silverstein's *Where the Sidewalk Ends*
- ☑ Marshmallows, soda crackers, or both
- ☑ A silly prize

How about a poetry recital by the cultured and highly literate young people of your group? Can't you imagine them now, just before the start of the meeting, sitting around discussing the finer points of Yeats or Shelley . . . debating the eschatology of the apocalyptic books of the Old Testament . . . you can almost see the rapturous delight written all over their highbrow, aristocratic faces when you announce your plan to have a poetry recital . . . wait . . . no, uh, maybe you were confusing your junior highers with that postgraduate philosophy class you walked into by mistake back during your college days.

Yet how about making a poetry recital into a spectator sport—maybe not an *extreme* spectator sport, but at least a *messy* sport? Into poetry, introduce the elements of speed and dry soda crackers. Ask a student to bring her lit text to youth group, find a poem, promise a small prize for whoever can

read it the fastest and with the most panache—and also with a mouth full of soda crackers.

You may want to bring small umbrellas for those in the front row.

After the game or the film clip, say something to this effect—

▶ **How many of you like to read poetry? How many of you write it? How many of you write poetry privately but don't admit it? Like it or loathe it, we're surrounded by poetry—at least in the music we immerse ourselves in.**

▶ **The lyrics of Easy Listening love songs to the moody raps whose bass riffs send every car at the intersection bouncing—these are all poetry. Poetry is in the greeting cards your grandma sends you on your birthday, in the nursery rhymes your little brother chants over and over, in the advertising slogans that promote your favorite products.**

▶ **And guess what? The Bible is full of poetry, too!**

Open the Bible and
Let the Show Begin!

Before the start of the session ask three members of your group to be prepared to read one of these three Proverbs—9:10 or 11:22 or 10:1. To make the reading more interesting, ask your readers to stay seated—until the moment arrives for them to read, when they should leap to their feet to read their verses and then sit down again, one after the other, like popcorn. At least it will keep the rest of the group guessing as to where the next Bible explosion will come from.

After the readings, tell the group that today's session is going to focus on the Proverbs—a book that uses the techniques of poetry to make its teaching expressive and memorable. Take a moment to explain to the group the foundation of Hebrew poetry in the Bible, using these three verses as examples.

24

▶ The whole idea of poetry is to use unusual language and words to paint pictures that help us to see things differently, or better. Poetry in our language is typically a *rhyming* poetry, like "Jack and *Jill* went up the *hill*." But not Hebrew poetry.

▶ So what makes Hebrew poetry *poetry* if it's not rhyme? Parallelism—the same idea being written two different ways, one way after the other. Like this, from Proverbs 9:10—

The fear of the Lord is the beginning of wisdom,
And knowledge of the Holy One is nderstanding.

Or look at these poetic lines this way—

The fear of the Lord	is	the beginning of wisdom
And knowledge of the Holy One	is	understanding

▶ This is parallelism at its simplest—repetition for emphasis.

▶ Proverbs 10:1 does the same thing, but contrasts one idea with the other:

A wise son brings joy to his father,

But a foolish son, grief to his mother.

And it gets even *more* interesting! Here's Proverbs 11:22:

Like a gold ring in a pig's snout

Is a beautiful woman who

shows no discretion

Look at it this way—

Like a gold ring	in a pig's snout
is a beautiful woman	who shows no discretion

▶ Again the two lines say approximately the same thing, but now a much more vivid illustration is being used.

▶ So guys, this pig-snout verse is a great one to memorize! With it stored in your mind, you'll have the perfect comeback whenever your girl-

friend disagrees with you. Say you're at the multiplex and want to watch an excellent police thriller—you know, lots of action and suspense and destructive car chases. Doris, meanwhile, wants to see a chick flick with lots of flowers and kissing and guys in Robin Hood tights.

▶ Armed with Proverbs 11:22, you say, "Honestly, Doris, don't you know what it says in Proverbs? *Like a gold ring in a pig's snout is a beautiful woman who shows no discretion.*" While she's standing flabbergasted in the middle of the movie center foyer, trying to work out if that's the nicest thing you've ever said to her or the most horrible, you just go ahead and buy two tickets to the action flick. And who said there's no point in memorizing the Bible! Of course, once she realizes you've compared her to a pig, she may question *your* discretion...and you may end up watching the movie alone!

Check Out the Lyrics
and put them to work

First your students need to pair off—and here's a fun way to do it.

What you'll need
☑ Slips cut from photocopies of the sheet **Modern Proverbs (and Some Not-So-Modern Proverbs, Too) (page 29)**

Before the session, photocopy the sheet and cut out the slips so there are as many slips as you'll have students. Give each student a slip—that is, half of a proverb—and instruct them to mingle until they find a person with the other half of their proverb.

For middle schoolers
Of gold rings and pigs' snouts

What you'll need

☑ Copies of the Staging Sheet **Of Gold Rings and Pigs' Snouts** (middle school version, page 30)

☑ Pens for all

Have each pair of students write their modern proverb in the upper-left box of their Staging Sheet **Of Gold Rings and Pigs' Snouts** (middle school version, page 30). Ask student pairs to discuss with each other what they think the proverb means and whether they agree with it. *But don't let them do the bottom row yet*—they'll write their own proverb a little later.

After you call your pairs back together in one group again, present the material on pages 72 and 75 of *Backstage Pass OT*. Make these points—

▶ **Proverbs are the teachings of wise people boiled down to their memorable essence. These biblical proverbs contain not merely knowledge, but wisdom for living life. Many of the issues touched on in the book of Proverbs are still relevant today.**

▶ **The big difference between the wisdom expressed in Proverbs and the wisdom from other sources is this: Proverbs' wisdom is based on the Lord—on loving him and obeying him.**

Now write your own proverb! What's a colorful way of saying, "Jealousy is bad"? Have a group brainstorm session and write on the whiteboard some ideas from kids for a proverb that conveys the message. Determine the best idea, then work together to forge a memorable proverb from it.

For high schoolers (root a little deeper)
Of gold rings and pigs' snouts

What you'll need

☑ Copies of the Staging Sheet **Of Gold Rings and Pigs' Snouts** (high school version, pages 31 & 32)

Introduce this Staging Sheet like this—

▶ **The rotting carcass of a large animal has been dragged out and left in the desert. Over time, and under the influence of the watchful vultures, devouring jackals, scavenging rodents, and hungry insects, all that's left are sun-bleached bones.**

▶ **What if time could do the same thing to your youth pastor's favorite sermon? What if 55 minutes of shouting, joking, ranting, and raving up in front of the youth room could be reduced to 15 seconds worth of pure wisdom?**

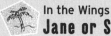 In the Wings
Jane or Solomon?

The book of Proverbs is a book of timeless advice for living life. So why not challenge your group about where they look for advice? Make these points.

▶ **Sometimes it's too much a part of the scene for us even to notice it, but the fact is that there are many people shouting advice to us on how *they* think we should live our lives.**

▶ **The advice pages of magazines, school friends, or, worst of all, horoscopes are all possible sources of wisdom for living. Trouble is, the advice they give isn't always very good. Sure,**

***Teeny-bopper's Monthly* recommended (with a coupon for 50 cents off!) the cream that got rid of your zits and revolutionized your life. But that doesn't mean you gotta follow what it says about what true romance is or that you'll only find the boy you should marry by answering its ten simple questions!**

▶ **The message of today's session is that the Bible provides wisdom for living that is appropriate and useful for us even though we live on the other side of the world centuries after it was written.**

Challenge your students to make the Bible their number-one source of wisdom for living.

▶ Well, that's exactly what proverbs are: pure wisdom, reduced and distilled over many centuries, from the teachings of some of the wisest people who ever lived, reduced and distilled over many, many years down to their bones—their barest essence. We still need sermons, but for every sermon I bet there's a proverb that captures its point in a few short lines. Fifteen seconds of wisdom—now *that's* the right length for a sermon!

Allow student pairs 10 minutes or so to work through the Staging Sheet **Of Gold Rings and Pigs' Snouts** (high school version, pages 31-32).

Then call the group back together for a feedback session. Referring to the first part of the Staging Sheet, say something like—

▶ What sorts of issues are addressed in these proverbs you've looked at? Are they at all relevant to life in the new millennium? In what way?

Listen for answers like *true beauty, greed, honesty*—timeless issues still highly relevant today.

Referring to the last part of this Staging Sheet, say something like—

▶ We've talked about various Sources of Wisdom. Let's try to rank them in order of importance or value.

Invite students to call out their rankings, track their responses on the whiteboard, and—if your group size permits it—spend three or four minutes trying to arrive at something of a conseusus.

▶ How did that Proverbs 9:10 verse help you to rate the different Sources of Wisdom?

▶ Listen for answers along these lines, and get the group's input about these and all responses:

▷ Any so-called wisdom that goes against anything God has directly said must be false. A magazine might say adultery is okay, but the Ten Commandments say otherwise.

▷ Any so-called wisdom that goes against what we already know about how God wants us to live must be false. If we oughta love even our enemies, then revenge will always be wrong—no matter what our friends say.

▷ Any so-called wisdom that comes from a source outlawed by God—whether it be horoscopes or fortune-telling or any other sorts of divination—must be false.

Take a Bow

Explain that the book of Proverbs is just one of a group of five Old Testament books called the books of Poetry and Wisdom. Ask if anybody can name the other four books in the group.

If they are struggling, give them this clue:

▶ The five books of Wisdom and Poetry fall exactly in the middle of the Old Testament.

There are 17 books prior to Job and 17 books after Song of Songs. If this clue is to be any help at all, your kids are gonna have to look at the table of contents in their Bibles—unless they actually know all 39 books of the Old Testament in order!

These are the five books in the Poetry and Wisdom group:

▷ Job—a book for those who are suffering

▷ Psalms—a book to help us express ourselves to God

▷ Proverbs—a book of timeless advice for living life

▷ Ecclesiastes—a book that's not afraid to look at the downside of life

▷ Song of Songs—a book that gives a God's-eye-view of sex

Make these points—

▶ These books—Job, Psalms, Proverbs, Ecclesiastes, and the Song of Songs—don't contain specific pronouncements from God like the books of the Law, or word-for-word messages from him like the books of the Prophets. These five books don't chart the progress of God's chosen people the Israelites like the books of history. In fact, two of these books—Ecclesiastes and Song of Songs—barely seem to have any time for God at all. So why are they even in the Bible?

▶ Because, incredibly, our gritty and often uncomfortable everyday lives are important to God. The issues these five Bible books talk about may not seem very religious, but they are immensely important to us as humans—

suffering • sex • how to build good friendships • how to be successful in life • what to do when you've blown it

▶ The books of poetry and wisdom are a wonderful example of the value of the Bible. It can speak God's truth to us in *every* area of our human existence.

Stage Door
Bible study: a new dance, right?

Demonstrate to your group how a *concordance* works. If they've got any kind of a youth or student Bible, chances are there's a modest concordance in the back. And a concordance is too good a tool to waste just because you don't know how to use it!

▶ A concordance is a Bible reader's power tool. With it you can find where a particular word appears in the Bible. Can't remember where a particular verse comes from but you know a couple words? Want to see what the Bible has to say about a particular subject?

▶ No problem. Look it up in the concordance. It works like an alphabetical index. You look up the word you want, and below it you find a list of references to verses that the word is in. Check the references till you find the verse you're looking for or till you run across a verse that has something interesting to say on the subject.

▶ Most of the time, the concordance in the back of your Bible is like a cordless screwdriver—not real big, but big enough for most jobs. But when the job's bigger, the tool needs to be bigger, too. That's when you reach for a twelve-volt construction drill—a *complete* or *exhaustive* concordance. Those tend to be huge heavy tomes, and usually the concordance in the back of your Bible will be all you need.

▶ Concordances are really helpful when you're struggling with issues and need to know what the Bible says about 'em. Suppose you're having hassles with your parents. Try looking up key words such as *father, mother, discipline, respect,* and *child* or *children* to see if your concordance leads you to any relevant verses.

Modern Proverbs
(and some not-so-modern proverbs, too)

MS & HS

• You're never properly dressed...	...without a smile.
• Don't put all your eggs...	...in one basket.
• Who serves two masters...	...has to lie to one.
• A stitch in time...	...saves nine.
• A bird in the hand...	...is worth two in the bush.
• Don't stand in the sun...	...if you've got butter on your head.
• Too many cooks...	...spoil the broth.
• Look before...	...you leap.
• People that live in glass houses...	...shouldn't throw stones.
• A golden key...	...opens all doors.
• Sticks and stones may break my bones...	...but words will never hurt me.
• Whenever you point a finger...	...there are four pointing back at you.
• Don't count your chickens...	...before they're hatched.
• No rose...	...is without thorns.

Of gold rings and pigs snouts

Staging Sheet

Proverb	What does it mean?	Do you agree?
(Write <u>your</u> complete proverb here!)		
Like a gold ring in a pig's snout is a beautiful woman who shows no discretion. —Proverbs 11:22		
Cast but a glance at riches, and they are gone, for they will surely sprout wings and fly off to the sky like an eagle. —Proverbs 23:5		
An honest answer is like a kiss on the lips. —Proverbs 24:26		
(As a group, think of an original proverb that expresses that jealousy is bad and write it here.)	**Jealousy is <u>bad</u>!**	

This handout is available for free at www.youthspecialties.com/store/backstage. From *Backstage Pass to the Bible* by Jonathan Brant. Permission to reproduce this page granted only for use in buyer's youth group. Copyright © 2002 by Youth Specialties.

30

Of gold rings and pigs' snouts

Part 1

HS

First, with your partner, choose one of these proverbs.

Proverb 1
Like a gold ring in a pigs snout is a beautiful woman who shows no discretion.
—Proverbs 11:22

Proverb 2
Cast but a glance at riches, and they are gone, for they will surely sprout wings and fly off to the sky like an eagle.
—Proverbs 23:5

Proverb 3
An honest answer is like a kiss on the lips.
—Proverbs 24:26

▶ Which particular **words** clue you in to what the proverb is all about?

▶ Any **images** in the proverb that strike you unusual?

▶ Try to explain in one sentence **what the proverb means to you**.

▶ Just **how relevant** do you think this proverb is to today's world? Why?

Of gold rings and pigs' snouts

Part 2

Staging Sheet

HS

Now check out this proverb, which some say is a summary for *everything* in the book of Proverbs.

The fear of the Lord is the beginning of wisdom, and knowledge of the Holy One is understanding.
—Proverb 9:10

But just where do you find this wisdom and knowledge? Below are several sources of wisdom—number them from 1 to 12 (or more), 1 being **wisest**.

___ Teachers

___ Horoscopes

___ Church leaders

___ Bible

___ TV

___ Advice columns in magazines and newspapers

___ Books

___ Advertising

___ Parents

___ School friends

___ Older brothers or sisters

___ Internet

___ Other ________________________________

___ Other ________________________________

The Old Testament Prophets

Use a video clip or a game for

Opening Act

Sports Bloopers the movie

You'll need this video–or *any* video of sports bloopers–for a game of What Happens Next?
(Most video stores have at least a shelf full of bloopers, sports and otherwise.)

Before the meeting find two or three genuinely comic and unpredictable clips. At your meeting divide your group into two or three teams (see **Divide into Small Groups Creatively!** on page 75) and warm up the teams by watching a few clips just for laughs. Then roll one of the good clips you selected earlier–and about ten seconds into it, freeze the video. Announce that each team has two minutes to (1) decide what happens next and (2) write an account to read aloud to the other groups. When the two minutes are up, each team reads its account. Then play the clip to its conclusion and award points according to who made the most accurate prediction. Play again with another of your good clips.

Play Your Cards Right
the game
What you'll need

☑ **A pack of playing cards**
☑ **Some way to stick cards temporarily to the wall–poster putty, tape, etc.**
☑ **Your group divided into two teams**
☑ **A small prize**

Divide your group into two teams, and stick two rows of seven cards to a wall (the cards' faces against the wall).

The game is simple. The top row of cards is for team 1; the bottom row, for team 2. The leader (that'd be you) turns over the first card (the one on the left) in each row. Now each team has to make a *higher or lower?* decision: if they believe the next card to the right will have a face value *greater* than the first, they say "higher." If they think the value will be less, they say "lower."

Say that the first card turned over is a two. The team will almost certainly say "higher"–and as long as the next card is at least a three, they're still in business. (It's when the first card is a seven or an eight that it gets dicey.) As long as a team guesses correctly, they keep on guessing. When a team guesses wrong, play moves to the other team. First team to guess all of its seven cards wins. Then shuffle and play again!

After the game or the film clip introduce the session with words to this effect.

▶ **So what do you know about the Old Testament prophets? Were they the kind of prophets with magical powers to see into the future? If only . . . they would have had a great life-they never would've been caught in the rain without an umbrella, never would've been turned down for a date, always known the answer before they asked the question. And they would've absolutely cleaned up at games like we just played.**

▶ **Yet predicting the future was only one small part of being God's prophets-and it wasn't a mere magic gift they had, either. They lived their lives in pretty much the same way as we do. And being a prophet put them in some pretty sticky situations.**

▶ **In this session we'll learn more about who the prophets were and what they did.**

Prophets Win Prizes

...and the million dollar question: who will win the World Cup in the year 2020?

Open the Bible and

Let the Show Begin

What you'll need

☑ A Bible

Have a group member read Amos 3:13-4:3 out loud. Then draw the group's attention to these two points about the passage that are typical of the books of the Old Testament Prophets.

▶ **Much of the passage is written with God speaking directly and in the first person–'I . . . '**

▶ **It's also written in the future tense–'will . . . ' It's about what God is going to do.**

▶ **At first sight much of the rest of what this passage says is completely unintelligible. Doctors' handwriting and the bright red scrawls your English teacher decorates your essays with are easier to understand! Well, don't give up hope! We're about to make this easier to understand.**

Check Out the Lyrics
and put them to work

For middle schoolers
Wild words from wild men

What you'll need

☑ Copies of the Staging Sheet **Wild Words from Wild Men** (middle school version, page 39)
☑ Bibles and pens
☑ Familiarity with the info on pages 82-85, 88 of Backstage Pass OT

Be prepared to present the information on pages 82-85 and 88 of *Backstage OT* about the Old Testament prophets. Make sure you cover these three key points.

▶ **The Old Testament prophets were a mixed bunch of men. Some of them were so odd, with their strange clothes, wild eyes and most of yesterday's breakfast still caught in their tangled beards that they would probably have been superb candidates for the loony asylum.**

▶ **Others were powerful or wealthy, and some were even members of the royal family. (When they weren't prophesying, they probably went around cutting ribbons at grand openings and trying to keep their love lives off the cover of the National Enquirer.)**

▶ **What they all had in common, whether they were nerds or nobles, was an intimate relationship with God and a deep understanding of what pleased and displeased God.**

▶ **If we want to understand what they said, we need to understand the people they were speaking to and what was going on during that the time.**

Illustrate this point, for example, with background info in *Backstage OT* about the Amos passage.

▶ **God didn't give his prophets a view of the future just for the fun of it or to impress pretty women. The predic-tions they made were always part of God's wider purpose in the world– either to warn his people, giving them time to change and avoid coming disasters or to give his people hope for the future after the bad things had happened.**

When you've finished this short talk, hand the Staging Sheet **Wild Words from Wild Men** (middle school version, page 39) to each student. They'll also need the use of a Bible. Give them five to seven minutes to complete the sheet. If students need a couple *real obvious* clues beyond the clues on their Staging Sheet, give 'em these.

▶ We don't know anything about the close relationships of the prophet Amos.

▶ Jeremiah was imprisoned in a muddy pit.

▶ Ezekiel was a priest and from a family of priests.

Here are the answers to share with your students when they're done.

Wild words from wild men

Write the initial of the prophet in the appropriate blanks. Use the clues at the bottom if you need help.

_E__ A priest and from a family of priests

_A__ We know virtually nothing about this prophet's close relationships

_J__ God told him he couldn't marry or have children

_D__ Young, handsome, and intelligent

_I__ Actually saw God

_E__ Declared that a valley of dry bones would come back to life

_D__ Saw more visions than said prophecies

_A__ Prophesied to the cows of Bashan

_I__ Married to a prophetess

_D__ Had three friends: Hananiah, Mishael, and Azariah

_J_ Imprisoned in a muddy pit

_A__ A shepherd

_E__ Made it a habit to act out his prophecies

_I__ Announced, "For to us a child is born, to us a son is given

_J__ Declared that one day God would make a new and better agreement

I	Isaiah
J	Jeremiah
E	Ezekiel
A	Amos
D	Daniel

Group Exercise

Does your group have time or interest for more along these lines? Throw out these Q's to spark discussion.

▶ **If one of these prophets was alive now and wandering around Lubbock [use your own town], what would he have to say about how people live in our town?**

▶ **What would he declare was wrong about the way people live in our town?**

▶ **What would he challenge people to do?**

▶ **Do you think our town's people would listen to him?**

For high schoolers (Greatest hits)
Wild words from wild men

What you'll need

- ☑ **Copies of the Staging Sheet Wild Words from Wild Men (high school version, page 40)**
- ☑ **Old newspapers or news magazines (Time, Newsweek, etc.), scissors, and glue**
- ☑ **Bibles**

Divide your students into work groups of three or four (see **Divide into Small Groups Creatively!** on page 75). Then hand out copies of the Staging Sheet **Wild Words from Wild Men** (high school version, page 40), scissors, glue, and two old newspapers or news magazines (like *Time* or *Newsweek*) to each of the groups. Make sure that each group also has access to at least one Bible.

Introduce the handout with this statement—

▶ **The prophet Amos-whose words are recorded in this book-was an uneducated shepherd and gardener when God called him to be a prophet. The way this passage is written, we can almost imagine the unimpressive but bold little prophet standing outside the gates of the city of Bethel and shouting out his message for all to hear.**

▶ **In your groups you'll look more closely at what he had to say and who he was saying it to.**

Allow your kids about ten minutes to work on the sheets individually or in small groups—then gather them together for feedback and discussion. Take the time to note what boxes have been checked and to see what pictures have been taken from the magazines.

Then do the following exercise as a group. Begin by saying—

▶ **Any of you dream of working in the media-magazine journalist, TV reporter, radio broadcaster? Well, today we're gonna be the production team for CBS Nightly News. (That would be the Canaan Broadcasting System). Our network has a reporter outside the gates of the city of Bethel, listening to what Amos is saying and** ready to summarize his words for viewers who are just coming in from work, sitting down in front of the TV with dinner, taking in the world.

▶ There's our reporter, standing in front of the camera in a pool of artificial light, one hand holding a microphone and the other hand pressed to her ear so that she can hear the voice of the anchorman back in the studio. Her report might start something ike this:

▶ *Yes, Bob. I'm standing here just outside the gates of the beautiful city of Bethel. Just a few moments ago a very strange young man (a shepherd, I believe) addressed some very unusual pronouncements to some very power-ful people. Quite honestly, I'll be surprised if he's still alive tomorrow morning after what he's just called the ladies of this fair city.*

▶ Any good TV news reporter will always take viewers to the *who? what? where? why?* and *how?* of a situation. So what do you think this reporter will say in the rest of her report?

Have the students call out their suggestions. Jot them down on a whiteboard and then work with your group to try to form them into a brief report. Any budding broadcast jour-nalists in your group? He or she may like to read the finished product, TV-like, to the rest of the group.

Be sure to leave your kids with these points firmly in their heads and hearts.

▶ In general, a prophet communicated God's viewpoint.

▶ The prophets spoke a *specific* message to a *specific* group of people.

▶ A prophet's message was usually a warning

I've got some luvley radishes this year

(as in this Amos passage) or a promise of hope after bad things had happened to the people.

Take a Bow

On this pageand the next page are a pair of diagrams that may help you explain some critical things to your students about the books of the prophets—**How We Tend to Interpret the Prophets** and **What the Prophets Were *Really* Talking About.** Be prepared to sketch these rapidly during your comments or scan these diagrams for use in your computer-pro-jection system or make an overhead transparency of them.

Sketch or show the diagram **How We Tend to Interpret the Prophets**, including the arrows that point from the books of the prophets out into the future and into the unknown. Say words to this effect—

▶ The way the Bible is usually organized can actually be confusing. Most books are generally arranged according to time—beginning at the beginning, middle in the middle, and the end at the end. (Cookbooks and dictionaries are notable exceptions.) But not the Bible!

▶ Take the prophets, for example: these books may be sitting at the very end of the Old Testament, yet the events

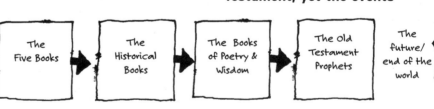

they describe occurred during and around the time of the historical books—you know, the books of Samuel, Kings, Chronicles.

▶ Here's one mistake people easily make about the prophets: just because the books of the Prophets come at the end of the Old Testament, we tend to imagine that most of these prophe-cies are about the end of the world, about good and evil, about dragons and beasts and earth-quakes and famines.

Now sketch or project the second diagram, **What the Prophets Were *Really* Talking About**—with the prophets *alongside*, concurrent with the history books, including the arrows between the prophets and the history books.

▶ **Most of what the Prophets said and wrote down was actually directed at the people living then (or shortly after) and about events that were occurring at that time. The prophecies were generally about the *near* future of the people they were speaking to, not to events that are still in *our* future. (Though, of course, a prophecy every now and then *did***

stretch out into the distant future to make a prediction.) And a lot of the prophecies foretold the coming of the Messiah, Jesus Christ.

▶ **Think of the books of the prophets running alongside the books of history, commenting on the events of that history. The prophets give us God's angle on what was going on. So to really understand and learn from them, it's best to study the prophets *alongside* the history books—and then ask ourselves, "What would God say about *our* times and the way we live *our* lives? What would an Old Testament prophet say to *us*?"**

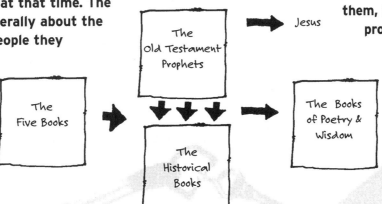

Stage Door
Really HEARING the prophets

Some of the writing in the books of the Old Testament Prophets is so beautiful and powerful that it practically begs to be read out loud by someone with the voice and the skill to do it justice.

Anyone with access to the Internet can hear the words of the Prophets read exquisitely by going to **www.audio-bible.com**. Scroll down on the left side till you find the book of Isaiah, then click on one of the chapters. For starters try Isaiah, chapters 9, 11, or 40.

Internet addresses do tend to change, of course. If this doesn't work, try the words *audio Bible* in your search engine.

In the Wings
Your money or your life!

What you'll need

☑ **Copies of the Staging Sheet Your Money or Your Life! (page 41)**
☑ **Pens**

Start with something like this—

▶ **Imagine a team of tiny Martians on a mission to Earth-a species so small that they can go anywhere on Earth without being seen. They keep hearing about Christian this, Christian that—so, to understand just exactly what a good Christian is, they visit churches. The only problem is that each church they visit gives them a totally different answer.**

▶ **In the first church they decide that clothing is somehow the badge of Christianity-specifically, males in suits and ties (three-piece suits a bonus), females in dresses that cover as much of them as suits cover their males.**

▶ **At the next church they're minds are changed quickly (and loudly): really good Christians apparently have to shout "Hallelujah!" and "Praise the Lord!" as they dance up the aisles, sweat buckets, and fan themselves with their church bulletins.**

▶ **The third church the Martians visit makes them shake their little green heads and change their minds yet again. Real Christians *here* have dour faces and impressive biceps formed not by weight training, but by years of carrying huge Bibles around.**

▶ **How many churches do you think the aliens would have to visit before they would finally conclude what Amos concluded-that the true lovers of God use their resources freely, and often firstly, to care for the poor and the needy.**

Hand out copies of the Staging Sheet **Your Money or Your Life!** (page 41) and allow the students a few minutes to fill in the three different columns. When they're finished, you may want to explore questions like these—

▶ **Which of these items do you spend the most on or the least on?**

▶ **Which do you think would be most important to the average wealthy person, who's got more money than he knows what to do with?**

▶ **Which do you think would be most important to Jesus if he were on Earth today?**

You can conclude the lesson with something like this—

▶ **If we're gonna get on line and in line with Jesus, we've gotta start using our money as we feel God wants us to. That means giving at least some of it to people who are in greater need than you are-starting now, and from now on.**

▶ **If you're starting to think that the priorities you listed may not be the best ones for you-or maybe even aren't the ones Jesus wants you to have-then join me in praying for God to help us to do better . . .**

waterlilies pic

your Monet or your life!

Wild words from wild men

Write the initial of the prophet in the appropriate blanks. Use the clues at the bottom if you need help.

___ A priest and from a family of priests

___ We know virtually nothing about this prophet's close relationships

___ God told him he couldn't marry or have children

___ Young, handsome, and intelligent

___ Actually saw God

___ Declared that a valley of dry bones would come back to life

___ Saw more visions than said prophecies

___ Prophesied to the cows of Bashan

___ Married to a prophetess

___ Had three friends: Hananiah, Mishael, and Azariah

___ Imprisoned in a muddy pit

___ A shepherd

___ Made it a habit to act out his prophecies

___ Announced, "For to us a child is born, to us a son is given"

___ Declared that one day God would make a new and better agreement

I Isaiah
J Jeremiah
E Ezekiel
A Amos
D Daniel

Need some clues? Try these . . .

▶ The priest from the family of priests made it his habit to act out his prophecies.

▶ See Daniel 1:4.

▶ One of Isaiah's key prophecies said, "For to us a child is born."

▶ The key prophecy of the prophet imprisoned in a muddy pit was that God would make a new agreement.

▶ The prophet considered young, handsome, and intelligent had three friends called Hananiah, Mishael, and Azariah.

▶ See Ezekiel 37:5.

▶ The prophet whose close relationships are unknown prophesied to the cows of Bashan.

▶ The prophet who actually saw God was also married to a prophetess.

▶ See Amos 1:1.

Wild words from wild men

Read Amos 3:13–4:3. You can take turns reading it aloud in your small group—or maybe you'll want to read it to yourself.

HS

There, finished reading? Good. Now check the items below that seem to characterize the sort of people Amos was talking about.

- ☐ Obviously religious
- ☐ Quietly religious
- ☐ On welfare (or the dole, or public assistance)
- ☐ Lazy
- ☐ Live in a duplex
- ☐ Live in a home with 3 bathrooms
- ☐ Boss
- ☐ Bus driver

- ☐ Powerful
- ☐ Plastic surgeon
- ☐ Employee
- ☐ Hard working
- ☐ Homeless
- ☐ Family of 5 with one car
- ☐ Wears a Rolex
- ☐ Wears clothes from a thrift shop (by necessity, not choice)

Amos said these people were in big trouble with God, particularly because of how they treated other citizens. See what Amos chapter 4 verse 1 says, then check the boxes that tell you what these meanies were doing wrong and who were they doing it to.

- ☐ Ignoring other people's suffering
- ☐ Being selfish with their wealth
- ☐ Forgetting God
- ☐ Not flushing after using the bathroom

- ☐ Maltreating the poor
- ☐ Being proud
- ☐ Kicking the cat
- ☐ Worshiping idols

When Amos was done telling people how sinfully uppity they were, he let 'em have it between the eyes with what God was gonna dump on them unless they changed their ways. See what threatens in chapter 3, verses 14–15, and chapter 4, verses 2–3—then put the Black Spot of Destruction next to those things the prophet predicted. (And was he ever ticked off . . .)

- ☐ Destruction
- ☐ Peace
- ☐ Demolition
- ☐ Celebration
- ☐ Judgment
- ☐ People taken prisoner

- ☐ The end of the world
- ☐ The end of cable
- ☐ Invasion
- ☐ Epidemic
- ☐ Prosperity
- ☐ Earthquake

Only 20 years or so after Amos relieved himself of this prophecy, Assyrian armies invaded the Northern Kingdom and the city of Bethel. They broke through the protecting walls (remember Amos 4:3?) and led the people away. Historical accounts and the art of the era reveal that the Assyrians led their prisoners all the way back to Assyria with hooks in their mouths! (Amos 4:2)

Your money or your life!

Guesstimate what you think Jesus, you, and the average
wealthy person spend on life's typical expenses.

	Jesus today	me	the average wealthy person
housing (including energy, water, trash disposal)	$	$	$
food (groceries and eating out)	$	$	$
clothing	$	$	$
giving to people in need	$	$	$
communication (including phone, cell phone, fax, Internet)	$	$	$
car (including fuel, maintenance, repairs, insurance, registration)	$	$	$
entertainment & recreation (cable TV, movies, videos, sporting events, CDs, concerts	$	$	$

The Gospels

Use a video clip or a game for

Opening Act

Forrest Gump the movie

Tom Hanks

Start 1:51 Forrest's run across America has attracted the media's attention—and made him a reluctant guru for a growing entourage of runners.
Stop 1:58 Forrest stops running and returns home

After the film clip make these points.

▶ Some people are so desperate for a leader that they'll follow almost anyone. Weird fads are started by equally weird people, but it usually isn't long before you discover that eating a raw turnip every day is bad for your social life–and then you begin to doubt anything the Turnip Guru says. (His pink sandals and combed nose hair don't help his credibility, either.)

▶ Today we'll look at the four Gospels–our prime source of information about the life and teaching of Jesus Christ.

▶ Ever since people started following Jesus 2000 years ago, a compelling reason to *stop* following him has never been discovered. In fact, today his followers are numbered not just in millions, but in billions–and they are spread throughout the continents of the world.

▶ In a phrase, Jesus was unique (*is* unique!) and the only person really worth following.

Human Freeze Frames

the game

What you'll need

☑ A photocopy of Freeze Frame Scenarios (page 46), cut into slips, one slip per student group
☑ These groups of student actors: a male and a female; two to five people; and two groups of any number of people

A dramatic exercise more convenient to compose than a skit or a mime, a Freeze Frame is a single scene frozen in time—like a snapshot or photo. Actors take up their positions and then stand motionless, allowing the audience to observe minutely what is taking place in that instant of time. The trick is to communicate as much as possible through positioning, posture, gesture, expression—with no movement whatsoever! Explain this to your students, then choose your groups:

▶ a male and a female

▶ two to five people

▶ two groups of any number of people

Now give each group the appropriate slip from **Freeze Frame Scenarios** (page 46). Groups shouldn't let others know their instructions.

Let them rehearse for a few minutes if they want to, or just have them "perform" improvisationally. After they've all seen each other's Freeze Frame, you now play director—assemble the four Freeze Frames so they obviously portray, together, the Nativity of Jesus, complete with parents, animals, Magi, and angels. (Okay, so all the historical characters portrayed by these students never actually converged like this . . . but it makes a great Freeze Frame.)

Have a really small youth group? Just have your whole group act out each Freeze Frame, one scenario at a time.

Open the Bible and

Let the Show Begin!

What you'll need

☑ A photocopy of the reading **So Who You Lookin' For, Huh?** (page 47)—or Bibles from which to read the two passages: Matthew 28:1-15 and 1 Corinthians 15:12-19

The reading on page 47 of the two Bible passages (Matthew 28:1-15 and 1 Corinthians 15:12-19) is from *The Message.* Use another translation of the Bible if you prefer. Try to get a couple good readers in your group to read this pair of passages—maybe a couple drama kids. Or read the passages yourself.

You'll notice that, whatever translation you read 1 Corinthians 15:12-19 in, Paul goes overboard on *raise* (or *rose, raising, raised,* etc.) and *death* (or *die, died, dead,* etc.) Before you read this passage aloud, tell your kids to do this (or something like this):

▶ When they hear a form of **raise**, they should stomp their feet (or applaud or stand and cheer or yell "Yo!"—whatever fits your group).

▶ When they hear a form of **die**, they should all moan (or lie down on the floor or yell "Bummer!"—again, whatever fits your group).

▶ When you're done reading, make a couple points, maybe in words like these.

▶ **Talk about overkill! Why does the Bible need four versions of Jesus' life? It's like a doting grandmother who carries around fifty gazillion photos of her drooling little grandson. I mean, if you've seen him all chubby cheeked in one photo, you've seen enough!**

▶ **Yet four accounts of Jesus' ministry is not really overkill at all. God inspired each of the four different authors to tell the story from their own perspectives and with their own unique emphases—which gives readers a far more rounded, three-dimensional picture of Jesus' life.**

▶ **It's like how the ju jitsu scenes in *The Matrix* were filmed. Dozens of cameras were positioned in a ring around the actors so that *every* angle of the leaping fighters was caught on film—a requirement for editing special effects into the fight scenes.**

▶ **The word *gospel*, you may know, means *good news*. And it's not merely the *good* news of the Cowboys or Packers winning on Monday night. The good news of the gospel is *very, very* good news—more like, "Did I mention that you've just won three million dollars in the lottery?" In fact, it originally meant something very specific—it was a messenger's good news that your troops had won the battle, had conquered, and that the time of fighting and of fear was over.**

▶ **The good news of the gospel is that Jesus conquered death by dying and then rising from the dead. Let's take a closer look at the resurrection of Jesus and the evidence that supports it. After all, just like Paul wrote to the Corinthians, the Christian faith *depends* on the historical truth of the resurrection.**

 In the Wings
This could get deep

Christianity is not a dead religion with a dead founder, but a living religion with a living Lord who can be encountered and known. This session, with its emphasis on Jesus as truly risen from the dead, is the perfect opportunity for those in your group that do not have a living relationship with the living Lord to enter into that relationship. Challenge your students to consider their faith. If they decide it's based on something other than a personal relationship with the resurrected Jesus, you can invite them to put that right. Lead them into that relationship in a way that's appropriate to your group and your context.

Check Out the Lyrics
and put them to work

For middle schoolers & high schoolers
The Great Resurrection Debate

What you'll need

- ☑ For yourself, the Staging Sheet **The Great Resurrection Debate** (page 48).
- ☑ Copies of **The Great Resurrection Debate** Staging Sheet pages for your students (same sheets for middle schoolers and high schoolers):
  - **Maybe Jesus Didn't Really Die at All!** (page 49)
  - **Maybe the Disciples Stole His Body!** (page 50)
  - **Maybe the Disciples Just Thought They Saw Jesus, But Were Actually Hallucinating!** (page 51)

This is a controlled debate about the evidence of the bodily resurrection of Jesus from the dead. On the table are three common *objections* to the resurrection—

▶ Jesus did not literally, physiologically die on the cross, but rather he experienced severe shock, trauma, coma, something of that sort.

▶ The reason Jesus' body was missing from the tomb was not a resurrection, but the theft of the body by his disciples.

▶ The disciples were merely hallucinating when they thought they saw the risen Jesus.

The details of these popular theories are outlined on the Staging Sheet **The Great Resurrection Debate** (page 48).

So pull that big black Stetson out of your closet, cock it at a ominous angle, and practice your most evil scowl—because now you're the bad guy. The arrogant know-it-all who thinks he has all the answers. The eternal skeptic who believes that the resurrection is no more than a pleasant, convenient fairy tale invented to keep soft-hearted, fuzzy-headed Christians from ever facing the harsh facts of life.

But don't worry—your brilliant, intrepid students are the posse, who will ride in just in time to save the day and make sure that truth triumphs in the end. To help them, each of the three **The Great Resurrection Debate** Staging Sheet pages raises an objection to the resurrection and presents the Christian response to it.

Introduce the debate with words to this effect—

▶ **Let's explore the evidence for the actual physi-**
cal resurrection of Jesus from the dead. We'll look at three common objections that skeptics of the resurrection raise to support their unbelief in this miracle—and we'll also explore Christian responses to those objections.

▶ **First, some facts that are accepted as true by most skeptics as well as Christians, by unbelievers and believers alike. These facts will form the boundaries of our debate. Most agree that—**

1. A man called Jesus really did live, that he was a teacher with a reputation as a prophet and miracle-worker, and that he was executed by crucifixion by the Roman authorities.

2. The tomb in which his body had been placed was later found to be empty—somehow, the body had disappeared.

3. It is a fact of history that during the months and years following his crucifixion, the belief that Jesus had been raised from the dead spread rapidly throughout the Mediterranean world—and, within a few centuries, deeply into Europe and Asia.

Divide the students into three work groups (see **Divide into Small Groups Creatively!** on page 75). Assign each group one of the objections, then give each group several copies of its corresponding Staging Sheet: **Maybe Jesus Didn't Really Die at All!** (page 49), **Maybe the Disciples Stole His Body!** (page 50), or **Maybe the Disciples Just Thought They Saw Jesus but Were Actually Hallucinating!** (page 51).

Give your kids five or ten minutes to familiarize themselves with their respective Christian response to whichever objection they have. When you call them together again, put on your best skeptic attitude—unrelentingly scientific, tenaciously antisupernatural. (Resist the attractive temptation to slip into the caricature of a rabid Christian hater—which implies to your students that unbelievers are enemies rather than sinners like themselves.)

As the Scowling Skeptic, present the first theory against the resurrection (Jesus didn't really die), then dare anyone to refute you. Accept questions and comments from other groups, too (including questions and comments from geuinely skeptical students). Move through the second and third theories in the same way.

Close the debate like this—

▶ During the past couple centuries, several unbelieving, skeptical lawyers have set out to disprove the resurrection—among them the 19th-century Harvard law professor Simon Greenleaf and the 20th-century lawyer Frank Morison—but, in the face of overwhelming evidence to the contrary, became convinced that Jesus' literal resurrection *did* occur and that Christianity was the only logical option. These lawyers typically believed on the basis of legal evidence that would stand up in a court of law.

▶ Of course, the strongest evidence for the resurrection is the phenomenal growth of the Christian church in the period shortly after Jesus' death, despite frequent and often severe persecution. The only viable explanation is that Jesus really did rise from the dead, and that it was because of his life and power that so many saw the truth of what his disciples preached.

Take a Bow

You may want to conclude with something like this—

▶ You could argue that the Gospels are the most important books in the world, because they are our primary source of information about the most important man who has ever lived.

▶ The life of Jesus Christ is the life that changed the world. Not only because now, 2000 years later, almost a third of the world follow him, but also because the influence his life and teachings have had on the other two-thirds.

▶ And it only helps that these books are simple and exciting to read—so dive in and read about the greatest man that ever lived!

Stage Door
Bible study: make mine creamed spinach, St. Mark, on the side, to go

Maybe you and your youth group are ready for a challenge like this—

▶ Imagine a family with this bizarre food fetish: they like to cover a whole table with all sorts of different foods. They each put on a blindfold, pick up a fork, and randomly stick it into some food, any food—goodness knows what kind. Then, still blindfolded, they place that fork o' food into their mouths. Just that one forkful. And that's dinner. Or breakfast or lunch.

▶ If you ate in such a family, sometimes you score with a forkful of steak or pecan pie. Other times you'd strike out with peas or spinach for weeks—maybe for many meals in a row. In either

case, you'd be constantly hungry and you certainly wouldn't be getting a balanced diet. Not to mention all that good food that would go untouched because you were so haphazard in your eating patterns.

▶ Is this sounding like the way we too often dip into the Bible? We read a couple of verses wherever it happens to have fallen open—then shut the Bible and get on with our lives. Not exactly a balanced Bible diet.

▶ Here's one way to fix a balanced and nourishing Bible meal—read an entire book of the Bible in a week or two or three. Don't bog down or dally around—just push on through the book. The Gospel of Mark is a good candidate for a read like this—only 16 chapters long, it covers the life, death, and resurrection of Jesus at a breakneck pace. There's hardly a break in the action, and Jesus is constantly on the move—places to go, people to see, enemies to fight.

▶ So here's the challenge: read Mark's Gospel before our next meeting. To read it in a week, all you gotta get through is two chapters a day and four on Sunday. C'mon, you can do it!

tripe and stuff

spam   menudo   pickled squid beaks   sautéed dandelion greens

Freeze Frame Scenarios

Group 1

One male, one female

Your Freeze Frame: the pride of young parents as they hold their first newborn baby in their arms.

Group 2

Two to five people

You're VIPs, movers and shakers, CEOs and producers and millionaires who are used to being obeyed, who are used to having everything done for you. Yet you've finally heard of someone who actually outranks you, and you've come a long way to meet this person.
   Your Freeze Frame: the moment that you meet this person. Try to demonstrate your pride even as you acknowledge the superiority of this person to you.

Group 3

Any number of people

Your Freeze Frame: inside a drafty old barn, you're the animals.

Group 4

Any number of people

Your Freeze Frame: you're a Gospel choir at the loudest and most joyful note in your most rousing song. This is the moment of ecstasy in your performance.

So who you lookin' for, huh?

Staging S...

From the apostle Matthew's version of the Gospel . . .

After the Sabbath, as the first light of the new week dawned, Mary Magdalene and the other Mary came to keep vigil at the tomb. Suddenly the earth reeled and rocked under their feet as God's angel came down from heaven, came right up to where they were standing. He rolled back the stone and then sat on it. Shafts of lightning blazed from him. His garments shimmered snow-white. The guards at the tomb were scared to death. They were so frightened, they couldn't move.

The angel spoke to the women: "There is nothing to fear here. I know you're looking for Jesus, the One they nailed to the cross. He is not here. He was raised, just as he said. Come and look at the place where he was placed.

"Now, get on your way quickly and tell his disciples, 'He is risen from the dead. He is going on ahead of you to Galilee. You will see him there.' That's the message."

The women, deep in wonder and full of joy, lost no time in leaving the tomb. They ran to tell the disciples. Then Jesus met them, stopping them in their tracks. "Good morning!" he said. They fell to their knees, embraced his feet, and worshiped him. Jesus said, "You're holding on to me for dear life! Don't be frightened like that. Go tell my brothers that they are to go to Galilee, and that I'll meet them there."

Meanwhile, the guards had scattered, but a few of them went into the city and told the high priests everything that had happened. They called a meeting of the religious leaders and came up with a plan: They took a large sum of money and gave it to the soldiers, bribing them to say, "His disciples came in the night and stole the body while we were sleeping." They assured them, "If the governor hears about your sleeping on duty, we will make sure you don't get blamed." The soldiers took the bribe and did as they were told. That story, cooked up in the Jewish High Council, is still going around.

—Matthew 28:1-15

From a letter the apostle Paul wrote to the Christians in ancient Corinth . . .

Now, let me ask you something profound yet troubling. If you became believers because you trusted the proclamation that Christ is alive, risen from the dead, how can you let people say that there is no such thing as a resurrection? If there's no resurrection, there's no living Christ. And face it—if there's no resurrection for Christ, everything we've told you is smoke and mirrors, and everything you've staked your life on is smoke and mirrors. Not only that, but we would be guilty of telling a string of barefaced lies about God, all these affidavits we passed on to you verifying that God raised up Christ—sheer fabrications, if there's no resurrection.

If corpses can't be raised, then Christ wasn't, because he was indeed dead. And if Christ wasn't raised, then all you're doing is wandering about in the dark, as lost as ever. It's even worse for those who died hoping in Christ and resurrection, because they're already in their graves. If all we get out of Christ is a little inspiration for a few short years, we're a pretty sorry lot.

—1 Corinthians 15:12-19

Both passages arre from *The Message* by Eugene Peterson, published by NavPress. Used by permission. © 1993 by Eugene Peterson.

The Great Resurrection Debate

Theory: Perhaps Jesus Didn't Really Die at All!

Here's what they say . . .

▶ *They say* Jesus didn't actually die on the cross but in fact just passed out from the pain and fatigue.

▶ *They say* that the length of time Jesus hung on the cross was much shorter than was normal. In fact, they do have a point: though it generally took criminals a few days to die, Jesus was on the cross for only a few hours.

▶ *They say* the Roman guards took Jesus down too early and that the next morning, after a chance to rest, he came to, stood up, and walked out of the tomb.

▶ *They say* that when he presented himself to his disciples, they were so surprised and so superstitious that they just assumed he had risen from the dead and started spreading that story.

Theory: Perhaps the Disciples Stole the Body!

Here's what they say . . .

▶ *They say* that after Jesus died on the cross and was placed in a tomb, his disciples came along and stole his body and then made up the story of the resurrection to make themselves seem more important.

▶ *They say* that the disciples might have overpowered the Roman guards or bribed them—or the disciples might even have robbed the tomb before the soldiers arrived to guard it.

▶ *They say* that, however the disciples managed it, they took the body and buried it in a secret place that only they knew about and then pointed to the empty tomb and claimed that Jesus had been resurrected.

Theory: Perhaps the Disciples Who Saw Jesus Were Just Hallucinating!

Here's what they say . . .

▶ *They say* that the disciples simply imagined that Jesus had been resurrected.

▶ *They say* that they wanted this to be true so badly that they actually began to hallucinate and to think that they had seen the risen Jesus.

▶ *They say* that once two or three people claimed to have seen Jesus, the rumor spread fast even though there was nothing to prove it, because so many people wanted to believe that it was true.

▶ *They say* that, once the idea had taken hold, the disciples did their best to spread it because it made them seem more important.

The Great Resurrection Debate
Maybe Jesus didn't really die at all!

Staging Sheet

MS & HS

If you don't believe that Jesus literally and actually rose from the dead, you have to explain why his tomb was found empty. And here is one way skeptics of Christianity do just that.

In a few minutes your group leader will present this theory to your group as if he or she actually believed this theory. Your job is to show just how unbelievable such a theory is. Work together in your group to make your case as convincing as possible. Each of you can speak up, or you can pick a spokesperson to speak for you.

The Theory

According to this theory, Jesus didn't die on the cross, but just passed out from the pain and fatigue.

As evidence, people who believe this argue that the length of time Jesus hung on the cross was much shorter than was normal for a crucifixion. And in fact, skeptics who say this *do* have a point. It generally took criminals on the cross a few days to die, but Jesus was on the cross for only a few hours.

They suggest that the Roman guards took Jesus down too early and that the next morning, after a chance to rest in the cool tomb, he regained consciousness, stood up, and walked out of the tomb.

Then when Jesus presented himself to his disciples, they were so surprised and so superstitious that they just assumed he had to have risen from the dead and started spreading that story.

The Response

▶ Jesus was crucified by tough and experienced Roman soldiers. They knew their jobs, and it's very unlikely that they would make the mistake of taking someone down off the cross who was not yet dead.

▶ The Bible records that when Jesus was stabbed in the side, both blood and water flowed out. Current medical science suggests that this is proof of death.

▶ Jesus had also been brutally beaten and tortured. Even without hanging on a cross for six hours, it's unlikely he would have recovered on his own without medical attention.

▶ Standard burial practice at the time involved wrapping the body like a mummy in cloth and sticky spices. And a boulder was in place across the door of the tomb. It's not likely that even a fit and healthy man (let alone someone who'd been beaten up) could have escaped—with no help—from the wrappings and moved the stone door.

If you don't believe that Jesus literally and actually rose from the dead, you have to explain why his tomb was found empty. And here is one way skeptics of Christianity do just that.

In a few minutes your group leader will present this theory to your group as if he or she actually believed this theory. Your job is to show just how unbelievable such a theory is. Work together in your group to make your case as convincing as possible. Each of you can speak up, or you can pick a spokesperson to speak for you.

The Theory

According to this theory, after Jesus died on the cross and was placed in a tomb, his disciples came along and stole his body—and then made up the story of the resurrection to make themselves seem more important.

People who believe this theory argue that the disciples may have overpowered the Roman guards or bribed them—or robbed the tomb of the body even before the soldiers arrived to guard it.

However they managed it, the disciples took the body and buried it in a secret place that only they knew about. Then they pointed to the empty tomb and claimed that Jesus had been resurrected.

The Response

▶ Body-snatching takes courage and planning. Yet the disciples were so scared and confused, all they could think about was how to keep from getting arrested or executed themselves.

▶ The highly trained Roman soldiers guarding the tomb would've had no difficulty defending the tomb from a disorganized handful of fishermen and tax collectors—especially since the guards knew their lives were at stake if they failed at their job.

▶ The tomb was found in perfect order—even the grave clothes were neatly folded. That doesn't really sound like the work of frantic grave robbers.

▶ It's believed that all of the disciples were eventually killed—martyred—for their faith in the resurrected Jesus. It's very difficult to believe that the very disciples who supposedly stole the body would've kept the truth a secret instead of confessing the hoax when their lives were on the line. Few scam artists are willing to die for a scam.

The Great Resurrection Debate

Maybe the desciples just THOUGHT they saw Jesus but were actually hallucinating!

MS & HS

If you don't believe that Jesus literally and actually rose from the dead, you have to explain why his tomb was found empty. And here is one way skeptics of Christianity do just that.

In a few minutes your group leader will present this theory to your group as if he or she actually believed this theory. Your job is to show just how unbelievable such a theory is. Work together in your group to make your case as convincing as possible. Each of you can speak up, or you can pick a spokesperson to speak for you.

The Theory

According to this theory, the disciples simply imagined that Jesus had been resurrected.

People who believe this theory say that the disciples wanted this to be true so badly that they actually began to hallucinate, thinking that they had seen the risen Jesus.

They argue that once two or three people claimed to have seen Jesus, the rumor spread fast even though there was nothing to prove it. Why? Because so many people desperately hoped that it was true.

They say that once the rumor had taken hold, the disciples spread it because it made them seem more important.

The Response

▶ Hallucinations are very individual experiences. Yet it's recorded that Jesus was seen by over 500 people after his resurrection. And in his letter to the Corinthians, the apostle Paul practically begs skeptics to go out and ask one of these many eyewitnesses (1 Corinthians 15).

▶ People who hallucinate are generally desperate for what they want to be true. The Bible is really clear that, far from the disciples *wanting* Jesus to be resurrected, the last thing in the world they *expected* was a resurrection from the dead.

▶ If Jesus' appearances were simply hallucinations, why didn't the Jewish or Roman authorities—who desperately wanted to prove that the resurrection hadn't happened—just go and get Jesus' rotting body and throw it down in some public place to prove he was really dead?

The Book of Acts

Use a video clip or a game for

Opening Act

Ace Ventura, Pet Detective the movie

Jim Carrey, Courtney Cox

Start 0:30 Ace Ventura (Jim Carrey) excuses himself to go to the bathroom, but he's really going to do some detective work **Stop 0:34** As they leave the party, Melissa (Courtney Cox) says, "I might have lost my job because of you."

Hand Detectives the game

At its best, this game can be a bonding activity that deepens relationships within your group. On the other hand, be fore-warned that it can also be a little intimidating—particularly for boys. Kids who find the game difficult often tend to laugh and horse around, destroying the effect for the rest of the group. So plan accordingly.

To begin, pair off your group. One of each pair is *Alpha*, the other is *Omega*. Then say something like this—

▶ **This game is about hands—and your partner's hands in particular. What's important here is not your senses of sight or hearing, but your sense of touch. You must shut your eyes and, in complete silence, explore your partner's hands with your hands. Are your partner's fingers long or short? Palms callused or soft? Any finger jewelry? Long nails? Try to find answers to all these questions using only your hands.**

Give the Alphas one minute to explore their partners' hands, then give the Omegas a chance. Then collect all the Alphas in one group and all the Omegas in another. Blindfold the Alphas. (If the group is large, in lieu of blindfolding them all you'll either have to trust your kids to keep their eyes shut or send them out of the room and bring them in one at a time.)

When the Alphas are blindfolded, have the Omegas stand in line, shoulder to shoulder in the middle of the room, and place their hands out in front of them. The blindfolded Alphas' assignment: to recognize their original partner using only the sense of touch in complete silence. They walk slowly down the line of Omegas, feeling each one's hands as they go past. They have only one chance to guess and can pass down the row of Omegas only once—so it's imperative that they concentrate! Once all of the Alphas have had a chance, let the Omegas take their turn.

After the film clip or the game, read Luke 1:1-4. Make these points—

▶ **History or biography writers have to be part detective. Luke, the author of a Gospel and also Acts, would've been a great detective because he had such a good eye for seemingly incon-sequential details. Wanting to make his two books totally convincing, he tried to be as accu-rate as possible with even the smallest of facts.**

▶ **Luke was probably a physician—a Gentile (not a Jew!) and possibly from the city of Antioch. He must've been a good doctor, because he's sup-posed to have lived to the age of 84. (Back then, that was old-old-old.)**

▶ **Luke was an eyewitness of much of what we read in Acts. And to be as accurate about the parts he *didn't* see firsthand as he was about the incidents he did, he probably traveled to the very sites to interview eyewitnesses and read government records and other documents. Most important, he made use of his friendship with principal players like Paul to get the inside story on all that had happened.**

Open the Bible and

Let the Show Begin!

What you'll need

☑ Copies of the Staging Sheet **A Reading in Acts** (page 56)—or just do the reading from the Bible—and at least 6 student readers

Before the session, arrange at least 6 students to read the Staging Sheet **A Reading in Acts** (page 56). Or they can read directly from Bibles—in which case divide the reading this way:

▶ **Luke the narrator**—verses 1-4, 6, 9-10

▶ **Jesus**—verses 4-5, 7-8

▶ **Disciples**—verse 6

▶ **Angels**—verse 11

After the reading explain that this session will focus on two aspects of verse 8—

▶ The outward spread of the gospel—even to the non-Jewish peoples (Gentiles).

▶ The power of the Holy Spirit made this possible!

Check Out the Lyrics
and put them to work

For middle schoolers
Pss . . . scoot over—the Gentiles just arrived!

What you'll need

☑ Copies of the Staging Sheet **Miracles in the Mediterranean** (page 57) for each student
☑ Bibles for all (or to share)
☑ Familiarity with pages 56-59 of Backstage Pass NT

Present the information about Acts found in *Backstage Pass NT* (pages 56-59). Emphasize these key points.

▶ The book of Acts tells the story of an explosion—the dynamic beginnings of the Christian church, complete with fireworks and spectacular results as the disciples proclaim the Good News about Jesus. And don't worry that Luke whitewashes history to make it look better than it actually was—he's also brutally honest about the early church's fights and failures.

▶ One clear purpose of Acts is to show how the Holy Spirit turned a group of bumbling disciples who couldn't organize their way out of a wet paper bag into powerful evangelists and church leaders.

101 things to do with a paper bag (wet or otherwise)

73. top hat

74. pull here to inflate / life jacket (does not conform to safety standard USP4561)

75. mmm, this is cosy / sleeping bag

▶ About halfway through the book, something rather shocking occurs—the kind of shock that makes your great-aunt swallow her false teeth or your pet goldfish forget how to swim. To their horror, all the good Jewish believers suddenly discovered—hold on to your socks now—that *God actually intended to allow non-Jews into the church.* The Jews had to scoot over and make room or else risk upsetting God in a big way. In fact, by the end of the book of Acts, non-Jews were a majority in the church—as they are today.

53

Then hand out this session's Staging Sheet **Miracles in the Mediterranean** (page 57), which helps your middle schoolers get a handle on the geographic spread of the gospel and the church. Save a few minutes for feedback from kids after they've worked on their sheets. Here's how your students' map should look:

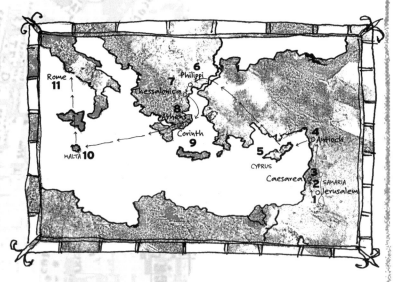

For high schoolers (Greatest hits)
Peter, Paul & (the son of) Mary

What you'll need

- ☑ Copies of the Staging Sheet Peter, Paul, & (the Son of) Mary (page 58)
- ☑ At least one Bible per group

Divide your students into six groups (see **Divide into Small Groups Creatively!** on page 75), and let each group choose one of these names (your students will see the significance of their group name once they start reading their assigned Bible passage, listed on the Staging Sheet)—

**Flaming Studded Tongues
Moshers on the Church Steps
Scatter Me
No Favorites
Purple Dreams
Roman Holiday**

Hand out a Staging Sheet **Peter, Paul, & (the Son of) Mary** (page 58) to each student, and make sure there's at least one Bible for each group if not for each student. Give them ten minutes to read their passage and fill out the questionnaire relating to it.

After ten minutes, call everyone back together for feedback and a chance to reinforce the key points. Referring to the map on their Staging Sheet, have each group tell where its Bible passage took place and who was involved. Plot the places on the map. As you do, you and your students will trace the spread of the gospel through the known world.

FYI, here are the answers to the Staging Sheet **Peter, Paul, & (the Son of) Mary** (page 58). The *How would you describe the Holy Spirit* question is, of course, pretty much subject to each student's perception—perceptions that are well worth exploring if you have the time.

 Stage Door
Tag along with Paul on a world tour

Page 59 of *Backstage Pass NT* gives the Bible references for Paul's three missionary journeys. Ask your students—

▶ **How would you like a chance to follow Paul around the Mediterranean Sea on one of his missionary journeys? You can take a virtual tour using computer multimedia resources such as *Encarta*. As well as making your schoolwork look oh-so-impressive, *Encarta* and other online encyclopedias make great Bible study tools.**

That might not be what Bill Gates and Co. had in mind when they developed them, but, hey, it works.

▶ **Here's how. Enter keywords like *Bible* and place names like *Corinth, Jerusalem,* or other cities that Paul visited. You'll find maps, pictures, soundbites and video clips that should help to make this journey come alive. You'll get a feel for the places and the cultures that he experienced, both as they exist today and as they were in Paul's day.**

Group	Where the action is	Actors
Flaming Studded Tongues (Acts 2:1-21)	Jerusalem	Peter and all the disciples
Moshers on the Church Steps (Acts 3:1-10)	Temple in Jerusalem	Peter and John
Scatter Me (Acts 8:1-8)	Samaria	Philip
No Favorites (Acts 10:23b-48)	Caesarea	Peter
Purple Dreams (Acts 16:6-15)	Philippi	Paul and companions
Roman Holiday (Acts 28:11-31)	Rome (no duh . . .)	Paul and companions

In conclusion, reinforce the key points of the session—

▶ **The book of Acts tells about the beginnings of the Christian church. The disciples start out as—well, wimps. But they end up as heroes, all through the power of the Holy Spirit. And in a surprisingly short time, they spread the Good News from Palestine throughout the Mediterranean world (which was pretty much all the world, to them). By the end of the book of Acts, non-Jews—that is, Gentiles—formed the majority of the church, as they do today.**

Paul on the move

Take a Bow

In the book of Acts we are introduced to many of the characters and churches that we'll meet again in the next section of the Bible—the letters. You can explain this simply to your students by saying something like this—

▶ **It's in the book of Acts that we learn about how Saul went from Christian killer to Christian. (Soon after his conversion he took the name Paul.) And about how Peter had a vision of his own, which completely changed the infant Jewish sect that was becoming known as Christianity. These two—Peter and Paul—are responsible for many of the letters in the New Testament.**

▶ **We also learn about the first gathering of Christians into churches in cities like Corinth, Philippi, Thessalonica, and Ephesus.**

▶ **Paul was a guy on the move. As you can see from *Backstage Pass NT*, page 62, he wrote a lot of his letters while on the missionary trail described in the book of Acts.**

 In the Wings

How the Holy Spirit makes jerks into giants

What you'll need

☑ Sheet of blank paper for each member of your group
☑ A 3-minute timer

Hand out the sheets of paper, one per student, with these instructions—

▶ **Using no tools other than your bare hands, transform the piece of paper I have given you into something new and original. You have three minutes. Go!**

At the end of the three minutes, ask some of the group members to show what they have made. Among the inevitable paper airplanes, you may find a few more artistic and original creations. Make this point—

▶ **The apostle Peter appears in both the Gospels and in Acts, but a major transformation in him takes place in between. Despite moments of brilliance (remember "You are the Christ!"?), he is usually impulsive—sometimes disastrously so (remember also that he denied Jesus the night before Jesus was killed).**

▶ **Fast forward—but to only a couple months later, when Acts picks up the story. Almost overnight, Peter becomes this fearless preacher, an anointed miracle worker, the guy who takes the gospel to the *Gentiles*, of all people.**

▶ **What causes transformations this dramatic? Well, Wonder Woman spun around, Superman disappeared into telephone booths to put on his red underpants, Batman made his own quick change in his Batcave. Peter? Lots of little things probably contributed, but the big reason is absolutely clear: it's the Holy Spirit who provides power like this.**

▶ **The Holy Spirit is still in the business of transforming lives. On what is left of your piece of paper—or on a fresh one if you can't write anything more on yours—write down one way you would like the Holy Spirit to come and transform you. Keep your transformed piece of paper and your request as a reminder that God helps us to change!**

A Reading in Acts

Acts 1:1–11

MS & HS

Characters

Luke (narrator)

Jesus

Disciples (2 or more students)

Angels (2)

Although this is pretty much straight from the Bible, it should be read dramatically.

LUKE: In my former book—that would be the Gospel according to Luke—I wrote about all that Jesus began to do and to teach until the day he was taken up to heaven, after giving instructions through the Holy Spirit to the apostles he had chosen. After his suffering, he showed himself to these people and gave many convincing proofs that he was alive. He appeared to them over a period of forty days and spoke about the kingdom of God. On one occasion, while he was eating with them, he gave them this command—

JESUS: Do not leave Jerusalem, but wait for the gift my Father promised, which you have heard me speak about. For John baptized with water, but in a few days you will be baptized with the Holy Spirit.

LUKE: So when they met together, they asked him,

DISCIPLES: Lord, are you at this time going to restore the kingdom to Israel?

LUKE: He said to them,

JESUS: It is not for you to know the times or dates the Father has set by his own authority. But you will receive power when the Holy Spirit comes on you; and you will be my witnesses in Jerusalem, and in all Judea and Samaria, and to the ends of the earth.

DISCIPLES: After he said this, he was taken up before their very eyes, and a cloud hid him from their sight. They were looking intently up into the sky as he was going, when suddenly two people dressed in white stood beside them, who said,

ANGELS: You of Galilee, why do you stand here looking into the sky? This same Jesus, who has been taken from you into heaven, will come back in the same way you have seen him go into heaven.

END

Miracles in the Mediterranean

Acts 1:1–11

It's a small world after all, it's a small world after all, it's a sma—

MS

Oh, so you know it too? The song that plays incessantly in your head for two solid weeks after you leave Orlando or Anaheim?

Well, it was a small world back in the first century. No matter where you lived then, your world was pretty much limited to where you could travel in a few weeks by foot or by sail. Here's a map of the world as it was known to those who lived around the fringe of the Mediterranean Sea—including the people who you read about in the New Testament.

Using the following references from the book of Acts, plot the spread of the gospel—from Jerusalem outward, all the way to Rome. The first place—Jerusalem—has been numbered for you. Put a 2 by the city (or region, if so noted) mentioned in Acts 8:4-5, a 3 by the city mentioned in Acts 10:1, and so forth. Then draw arrows that trace the progress of Christianity from place to place, as it worked its way through the Mediterranean world.

1 Acts 1:12

2 Acts 8:4-5 *(a region)*

3 Acts 10:1

4 Acts 11:25-26 *(careful—there are two cities by this name, one near the northeast corner of the Mediterranean Sea and the other farther to the west of the first one. Here Luke is writing about the first one.)*

5 Acts 13:4 *(you want the island)*

6 Acts 16:12 *(you want the city mentioned in this verse, not the region)*

7 Acts 17:1 *(where the synagogue was)*

8 Acts 17:15

9 Acts 18:1

10 Acts 28:1 *(another island)*

11 Acts 28:14

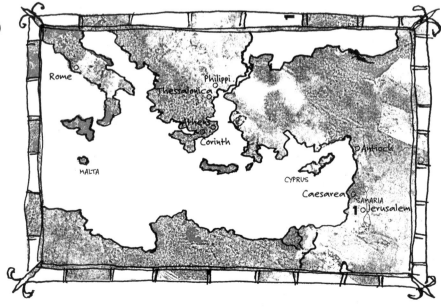

Peter, Paul & (the son of) Mary

Okay, you should already be part of a group. (If not, form six groups—quick!—and choose one of the group names below.) Next to your group name are Bible verses you need to read together in your group.

HS

Flaming Studded Tongues—Acts 2:1-21
Moshers on the Church Steps—Acts 3:1-10
Scatter Me—Acts 8:1-8

No Favorites—Acts 10:23b-48
Purple Dreams—Acts 16:6-16
Roman Holiday—Acts 28:11-31

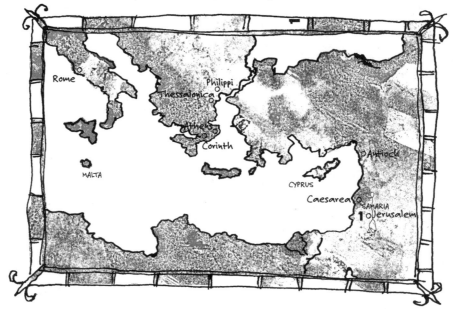

Where do the main events of your passage take place? (check a box that makes sense to you)

- ☐ Rome
- ☐ Philippi
- ☐ Caesarea
- ☐ Samaria
- ☐ Jerusalem
- ☐ The temple in Jerusalem

What else about the city does your Bible passage tell you?

What disciples or Christians were actors in these events? (check a box that makes sense to you)

- ☐ Philip
- ☐ Peter and all the disciples
- ☐ Peter
- ☐ Paul and companions
- ☐ Peter and John
- ☐ Bart and Lisa

So how would you describe the Holy Spirit, based on the events in the Bible passage you read? (check a box that makes sense to you)

- ☐ Water Boy *(not a lot to do, really)*
- ☐ Special teams *(not always involved, but pops up at key moments)*
- ☐ Offensive Line *(real hard worker)*
- ☐ Coach *(huge influence, but it's all behind the scenes)*
- ☐ Quarterback *(the number-one playmaker, star of the show)*
- ☐ Sorry, but this football stuff doesn't work for me. Here's what I'd call the Holy Spirit:

_____

The New Testament Letters

Use a video clip or a game for

Opening Act

Fierce Creatures the movie

John Cleese, Jamie Lee Curtis, Kevin Kline

Start 0:12 Cut to zookeepers holding small animals as they process through the zoo
Stop 0:18 Rollo Lee (John Cleese) tries to resume the phone conversation: "Hello? Hello?"

Delayed Answer Quiz the game

What you'll need

- ☑ **Three or four students, chosen carefully (see quiz instructions)**
- ☑ **Student timer with a stopwatch**

You need to choose three or four contestants for this quiz competition.

Now, then. The mature, godly thing to do in a situation like this is to invite the good-natured extroverts to play—the kids who don't mind a laugh, even at their own expense. This is undoubtedly the path you will choose. Of course, despite the fact that this quiz game is an enticing opportunity to put one or two of your group's opinionated know-it-alls in their places—this is reason to *not* use this approach. Only fiendish youth workers would stoop to this, right?

Right. Let this explanation dissuade you from using this fiendish plan. Certain diabolical youth workers could tempt student know-it-alls into volunteering by playing the quiz up as a test of intellect—a real chance to let one's brilliance show, eh? Then said fiendish youth workers would revel in the contestant's discombobulation, as the latter discovers—alas, too late—that, while the task *does* test intelligence, it leaves even the winner smelling not much like a rose.

So of course we'll all assume that you—

choose those gentlestudents who enjoy being the brunt of mild humor. Anyway, here's how the game works: ask the 3 or 4 contestants to leave the room and wait where they can't hear what's happening. Bring them in one at a time and explain the rules of the quiz to them. They will be asked 12 simple questions, and the winner will be the contestant who can answer all the questions in the shortest period of time without either making a mistake or smiling or laughing. You should have a student with a stopwatch keeping track of each contestant's time.

Oh, yeah—and the *last* rule is that contestants must always answer *one question late*. In other words, they can't answer the first question till they've heard the second question, nor the third question till they've heard the second, and so on.

Here are the questions.
1. **What is the color of grass?** (Remember, no one should answer when you ask this question.)
2. **What color are your teeth?**
3. **What is your full name?**
4. **Who do you love most in all the world?**
5. **If you had a pet cockroach what would you call it?**
6. **What do you put on your toothbrush?**
7. **What's your favorite spread for toast?**
8. **What do you wash your hair with?**
9. **What do you really want for your birthday?**
10. **In what year was your eighth birthday?**
11. **When did you last take a shower?**
12. **When did you last play with your Barbie doll** (for guys) / **Mighty Morphin Power Ranger** (for girls)?

When you're done with the video clip or the game, then take things this direction—

and to garnish, a smidge of toothpaste

▶ **Look at the confusion and sometimes hilarious misunderstandings that can arise *when we don't have all the facts*–either because we don't hear both the question and the answer (as in the quiz) or because we don't correctly understand the other person's situation (as in the film clip).**

- ▶ This session is about the New Testament Letters—which are not textbooks, but genuine letters written to real people, usually in answer to specific questions or to address specific situations. Just as in *Fierce Creatures* [or the delayed-answer game], things get confused if we don't know the questions or don't have a complete picture of the situation.

- ▶ Confusion and misunderstanding about these biblical letters are usually avoided if we read them with an eye toward getting the big picture.

Use the following exercise for five min-utes or so to get your students thinking about how they should be thinking when they read the New Testament Letters.

Explain that you are about to read two excerpts from letters—not Bible letters, just letters. Read the excerpts one at a time, asking the following questions after each one.

- ▶ Who do you think was writing this letter?

- ▶ Who do you think it was written to?

- ▶ What situation might have caused them to write like this?

  - ▷ "... I know you dated him and I know he treated you really badly, but he's changed now—honestly, he's so sweet—and I just know things are going to work out well for us ..." *(possibly a teenage girl writing to her best friend soon after she has started dating her friend's ex-boyfriend)*

  - ▷ "... I don't know why you're both so mad at me. It's not like I ever wanted to be an engineer or anything. What use is math to a professional surfer, anyway? Besides, even Einstein flunked math in high school ..." *(possibly a high schooler writing to parents after having flunked a math class)*

- ▶ So as you read the New Testament letters, ask these same questions—who's writing this letter, who was the letter's intended readers, why did the writer write it, what was the situation? This way we'll have a much better chance of understanding and correctly interpreting the teaching these letters hold.

Open the Bible and

Let the Show Begin!

What you'll need
☑ A student reader

Find a student who will read Galatians 1:1-9 for the whole group. Then, putting to practice the suggestions you made earlier in the session, ask these three questions—and encourage the students to answer them based *only* on what has just been read.

- ▶ **Who do you think was writing this letter?** *(Paul, an apostle. Sounds like someone with authority—maybe a teacher or leader.)*

- ▶ **Who do you think it was written to?** *(The churches in Galatia. Sounds as if the churches were getting off-track somehow.)*

- ▶ **What situation might have caused him to write like this?** *(A false gospel, whatever that is, was being preached by unknown teachers in Galatian churches.)*

Point out that a lot can be discovered through careful, thoughtful reading of the New Testament Letters—and even *more* can be learned if we take advantage of other resources. (See the **Stage Door** sidebar for some of these.)

it says here, shake well before application

d'you think this'll do?

Check Out the Lyrcis
and put them to work

For middle schoolers & high schoolers
No junk mail here

What you'll need

☑ Copies of the Staging Sheet **No Junk Mail Here!** (page 64) for each student

☑ Familiarity with pages 62-63 of *Backstage Pass NT*

Start by presenting basic information about the New Testament letters. Use pages 62-63 of *Backstage Pass NT*. Say something like—

▶ **Of the New Testament's 27 books, 21 of 'em are letters—from Romans to Jude.**

▶ **Thirteen of these letters were written by the apostle Paul. The rest were written by the apostles Peter, John, James, and others.**

▶ **Some were written to groups—churches or geographic regions—and others to individuals:**

  ▷ **Paul's letters are named for the people *he wrote them to*—Corinthians was written to the church at Corinth, Galatians to the Christians in Galatia, Ephesians to the church in Ephesus, letters to Paul's buddies Timothy and Titus, and so on.**

  ▷ **After the letter to the Hebrews, the letters are named by *who wrote them*—letters from James, Peter, John (a whopping 3 letters by him), and so on.**

▶ **What order are the letters in? Well, it has nothing to do with their relative importance or when they were written. Generally, they're simply organized, this way: Paul's letters come first (his letters to groups followed by his letters to individuals), then come letters written by other people.**

Now hand out copies of the Staging Sheet **No Junk Mail Here!** (page 64) and allow them ten minutes to match the quotes to the letters.

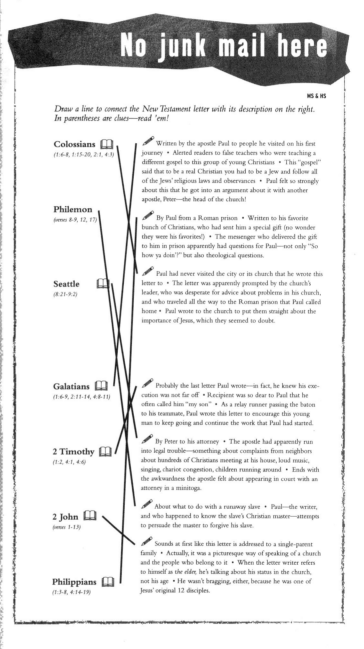

After this time call them back together for a time of feedback and to establish the correct answers. Need answers to the Staging Sheet? See the thumbnail above.

Take a Bow

At the close of this session communicate these key points to your students.

▶ At the risk of stating the obvious, the New Testament letters are just that—letters. Most of the writers would have received good grades in English class (or rather Greek class) because they follow all the ancient customs of letter writing. Paul, of course, would have aced the class (thanks to his debate club experience), but then you'd expect nothing less from the university-educated highbrow. (There were probably times when he just irked Peter and the other blue-collar apostles.) Yet Paul's letters weren't just exercises in logic—they were usually written to answer specific questions or in response to specific problems or situations.

▶ Remember, these are real letters we're reading. Just because they're *old* letters doesn't mean they're a religious textbook. In fact, it's probably a mistake to think that every detail in every letter ought to be done all the time, in every situation. This kind of interpretation leads only to confusion and pointless doctrinal debate in the churches. Of course, there are plenty of general obser-vations and truths in the letters that *are* applicable to all times and everywhere, too.

▶ You'll figure out the difference when you remember to read the Bible in terms of *past*, *present*, and *future*. What did this passage mean to those to whom it was *first written*? What does it mean to me *now*? What should I think or do differently *in the future* because of what this passage says?

Stage Door
Bible study: to whom, by whom, what about, why?

To get the most out of reading a New Testament letter, you need to learn as much as possible about its background. Who was it written by? Who was it written to? What kind of issues was it written to address? *Backstage Pass NT* gives some basic clues, but there are lots of other resources, too, that will help you dig deep and get the inside story.

Study Bibles are a great start. There are lots of 'em out there—even Bibles particularly for students, which usually go by the name of *student* or *youth Bibles*. They usually provide an introduction to each book—which explains the situation surrounding the writing of the book. Many student and teen Bibles do this well. The *New Student Bible* (Zondervan), available in the New International and the King James Versions, conveys the spirit as well as the historical details behind each Bible book; it's great for older adolescents. The *Teen Devotional Bible* (NIV, also published by Zondervan) does the same thing, in a briefer but zingier way, for younger teens.

In the Wings
A lot of nautical miles just for advice

You can use the letter to the Colossians to help your students see what it looks like to accept help and advice from more mature Christians. Say something like this—

▶ A man named Epaphrus shows up in the letter to the Colossians. He probably became a Christian thanks to Paul's teaching—and he apparently became a successful evangelist and church leader, with responsibility for an entire region. In Paul's letter to the Colossians we learn that Epaphrus traveled all the way to Rome in order to speak to the apostle Paul and ask his advice.

▶ Transportation wasn't the same then as it is now, of course. Epaphrus's trip wasn't a couple of hours luxuriating in business class with free champagne and movies—it was several weeks on a camel's hump, sharing its bad temper, bad breath, and bad gas. Or in a rickety cart behind an equally gassy mule that bumped him mile after mile to Rome. (Of course, a sea voyage was part of the trip, too.)

▶ But he finally got to Rome and got the advice and help he needed from Paul. An important part of growing up as a Christian is being humble enough to know when you need help—and then doing whatever is necessary to find it.

If your group is so inclined, ask them to voice or write three questions they'd like to ask an older Christian if they knew they'd get taken seriously. You can use this information to later invite such adults to speak to the group (maybe for a special "Saints Answer Your Questions!" meeting) or encourage the kids to take their questions to mature Christians they trust.

MS & HS

Draw a line to connect the New Testament letter with its description on the right. In parentheses are clues—read 'em!

Colossians 📖
(1:6-8, 1:15-20, 2:1, 4:3)

Philemon 📖
(verses 8-9, 12, 17)

Seattle 📖
(8:21-9:2)

Galatians 📖
(1:6-9, 2:11-14, 4:8-11)

2 Timothy 📖
(1:2, 4:1-2, 4:6)

2 John 📖
(verses 1-13)

Philippians 📖
(1:3-8, 4:14-19)

🖋 Written by the apostle Paul to people he visited on his first journey • Alerted readers to false teachers who were teaching a different gospel to this group of young Christians • This "gospel" said that to be a real Christian you had to be a Jew and follow all of the Jews' religious laws and observances • Paul felt so strongly about this that he got into an argument about it with another apostle, Peter—the head of the church!

🖋 By Paul from a Roman prison • Written to his favorite bunch of Christians, who had sent him a special gift (no wonder they were his favorites!) • The messenger who delivered the gift to him in prison apparently had questions for Paul—not only "So how ya doin'?" but also theological questions.

🖋 Paul had never visited the city or its church that he wrote this letter to • The letter was apparently prompted by the church's leader, who was desperate for advice about problems in his church, and who traveled all the way to the Roman prison that Paul called home • Paul wrote to the church to put them straight about the importance of Jesus, which they seemed to doubt.

🖋 Probably the last letter Paul wrote—in fact, he knew his execution was not far off • Recipient was so dear to Paul that he often called him "my son" • As a relay runner passing the baton to his teammate, Paul wrote this letter to encourage this young man to keep going and continue the work that Paul had started.

🖋 By Peter to his attorney • The apostle had apparently run into legal trouble—something about complaints from neighbors about hundreds of Christians meeting at his house, loud music, singing, chariot congestion, children running around • Ends with the awkwardness the apostle felt about appearing in court with an attorney in a minitoga.

🖋 About what to do with a runaway slave • Paul—the writer, and who happened to know the slave's Christian master—attempts to persuade the master to forgive his slave.

🖋 Sounds at first like this letter is addressed to a single-parent family • Actually, it was a picturesque way of speaking of a church and the people who belong to it • When the letter writer refers to himself as *the elder*, he's talking about his status in the church, not his age • He wasn't bragging, either, because he was one of Jesus' original 12 disciples.

The Book of Revelation

Use a video clip or a game for
Opening Act

Contact the movie

Jodie Foster, David Morse
Contact the movie

Start 0:00
Stop 6:30 When young Ellie asks, "Could we talk with Momma?" her father replies, "I don't think even the biggest radio could reach that far."

After the film clip say something like—

▶ **The created universe is more vast and more wonderful than it's possible for our frail minds to comprehend. But Revelation (as in, the Revelation of Jesus Christ—you know, the *revealing* of him) is the final book of the Bible, taking us beyond even the limits of the created world, further than the largest telescope or radio could ever reach, even outside of time, into the realm of heaven and right to the throne of God.**

space...
the next-to-the-final frontier

can we go back? I think I left the oven on

Mystery Words
the game
What you'll need

☑ **Slips cut from photocopies of the Staging Sheet Mystery Words (pages 70-71)**
☑ **30-second timer**

Divide your group into two teams (see **Divide into Small Groups Creatively!** on page 75), and give them each a Revelation-inspired group name: Locusts versus Angels, Swords versus Scrolls, Lambs versus Horses, Stars versus Fire—you get the idea. Then explain these basic rules.

▶ **The object of the game? A player takes a Mystery Word slip and must describe that word to his teammates within 30 seconds—though without saying the letters of the alphabet, proper names, or Forbidden Words. Forbidden Words are also listed on the slip.**

▶ **If your teammates are able to guess the word you're trying to describe within 30 seconds, then your team will receive a point. If they cannot guess it, or if you use one of the Forbidden Words, your team receives *no* points.**

Now separate the two teams so that they're standing in two straight lines, shoulder to shoulder, teams facing each another. The Locusts (or whoever) nominate one of their own to receive one Mystery Word slip, which also lists the Forbidden Words. The player comes out from her line and faces her fellow Locusts, with her back to the Angels. She holds the slip so that Angels, her opponents, can see both the Mystery Word and the Forbidden Words over her shoulder—in this way the Angels referee the round to ensure that none of the Forbidden Words are used. But they can't interrupt unless the rules are broken. Once the first player's turn is over, play moves to the Angels, one of whom choose a Mystery Word slip, and play continues in the same manner.

After you've played through all 10 of the Mystery Words (five per team)—or after 10 minutes, whichever comes first—move straight on to the next section of this session.

Open the Bible and

Let the Show Begin!

☑ Copies of the Staging Sheet A Reading from Revelation (page 72)
☑ Two student readers

Before the session begins, recruit two students to read the Staging Sheet **A Reading from Revelation** (page 72), which is simply Revelation 1:9-20, verbatim from the Bible.

After the reading, explain to your group that this session focuses on the final book of the Bible, Revelation. Then make these general introductory points—

▶ **This John guy is the author of Revelation, and probably the apostle John—disciple of Jesus and author also of the Gospel of John and the letters 1, 2, and 3 John. By the time he wrote Revelation, he was probably an old man.**

▶ **And forget Alcatraz—back in John's time, the island you didn't want to get sent to was Patmos. This little speck of rock and dust was where the Roman authorities sent their most feared prisoners—and it's where John was at during the time of his visions. He wasn't there for being some kind of arthritic Jesse James, who robbed senior citizens of their pensions. John was imprisoned on Patmos apparently because he was a leader of the Christian church.**

▶ **Right up front in Revelation, we're told that John wrote the book primarily for churches he had been working with—but it was probably also intended to be read by the wider Christian community. And John would probably be surprised to know it's still being read by us almost two millennia later!**

▶ **John wrote Revelation during a time of increasing persecution of the Christian church by the Roman emperors. You can tell from what he wrote that he hoped the book would strengthen and bring hope to his Christian brothers and sisters during this difficult and frightening time.**

Check Out the Lyrics
and put them to work

For middle schoolers & high schoolers
Apoca-*what?*

Point out that Revelation has probably caused more confusion, misunderstanding, and argument among Christians than any other book of the Bible—and with good reason, because it's really a bear to understand.

And here are just two reasons *why* it's a bear—

STYLE OF WRITING

▶ **The writing style in the book of Revelation is called *apocalyptic* writing, which is kinda like a cartoon in writing. Revelation has its own rules—things happen in Revelation that simply aren't possible in the real world as we know it.**

Harry "The Hammer" O'Flacherty

John "The Apostle" ben Zebedee

Mickey "Monster Face" McGraw

Patmos

▶ You've seen this in cartoons—you know, like Daffy Duck getting shotgunned in the head at point-blank range. Result? Burnt feathers and a missing duckbill—and he's back on his webbed feet for more of the same a minute later. Okay, so cartoons are off the wall in some ways—but they're true to life in other ways. We can relate to Bart Simpson's feelings and struggles even though his life and experiences are far from normal.

▶ Because we have grown up watching cartoons, we know how to understand them and what they mean. The original readers of Revelation—that is, the churches John first sent the book to—understood his apocalyptic style of writing in the same way we've learned to understand cartoons. For this reason, all the locusts and creatures and bowls and trumpets and deaths and Lambs and seals and prostitutes—they sound just plain bizarre to us, but John's original readers weren't confused. They were used to writing like this, the same way we're used to the improbabilities of cartoons.

THE NEED FOR A CODE

If you played **Mystery Word** earlier in this session, then remind kids how difficult it was to describe some of those words when you were prohibited from using some very appropriate words. John had the same problem when he was writing Revelation.

▶ John wrote Revelation kinda in code—not to be clever or to make his book difficult to understand, but to carefully avoid saying anything that would make the Roman authorities more suspicious than they already were of Christians. So John was very thoughtful about what he said, and even disguised some words so the real meaning would not be understood by outsiders.

▶ We're pretty sure about some of these words. For example, it's widely accepted that *Babylon* in Revelation is John's code for *Rome*. Other Revelation terms might have been used as code, too—maybe to disguise the names of Roman emperors—but we're not so certain of these.

▶ What's important to remember is that John had to worry about offending the Roman authorities, so he was forced to disguise some of what he wrote behind a kind of code.

So John's *writing style* and *his need for code* are just two reasons why Revelation is on the difficult side to understand.

For middle schoolers
Dancing through Revelation

What you'll need

☑ Old newspapers
☑ Tape

At this point, middle schoolers will probably have had their fill of Revelation. Actually, they probably had their fill of Revelation about an hour before they walked in the door, and you've been living on borrowed time ever since. Anyway, this section of the session is less intense, with an opportunity to let off some steam.

Announce an indoor snowball war! When the kids stop yelling, tell them the snowballs will be paper. Divide your

Discussion starter

Will there be dogs in heaven?

We all have a rather hazy idea of what heaven will be like and what our everlasting life there will involve. If we're honest, we might have to admit that we're not at all sure that we're excited by the thought of worshiping 7/24 for millions of years. To get the group members talking about their views of heaven, ask questions like these—

▶ **What do you think you'll do in heaven?**

▶ **What are you particularly looking forward to?**

▶ **Is there anything you are *not* particularly looking forward to about heaven?**

▶ **Do you think there is anything that you will *not* be allowed or able to do in heaven?**

▶ **Do you think there is anything you do here on earth that you will miss doing in heaven?**

group into two teams (see **Divide into Small Groups Creatively!** on page 75) and give each a stack of old newspapers. While they're crumpling paper into snowballs, you can take some sheets of newspaper and some scotch tape to make two cone-shaped hats, like dunce caps.

Set up chairs in two straight lines facing each other across a small strip of No Man's Land. Place one more chair about two yards behind each row. When everything's ready, explain how this war will be fought—

▶ **Each team chooses one player, who will wear the cone-shaped hat and sit on his or her team's back chair. Hat-wearer, you won't be throwing paper balls or catching them—in fact, you can't use your hands at all, so just sit on 'em!**

▶ **For the rest of you, the object of the game is to knock the hat off the head of the other team's hat-wearer—and you do this by throwing paper balls at the hat. Of course, at the same time you should also defend your own hat-wearer by batting down the enemy's shots. All of this, while sitting—and staying!—in your chair.**

When the teams are seated, let the war begin! If the room's not too big, paper balls can just get recycled as they're thrown back and forth. If too many balls wind up out of reach, you can declare a short truce and allow each team a few seconds to collect all the paper balls lying on its side of the room.

Once a winning army has been declared—or you've played a few rounds of this game—hand out Bibles to the group and read Revelation 19:11-21 like this:

▶ **Winners** read verses 11-16 aloud, together; then

▶ **You**, the leader, read verses 17-18; then

▶ **The defeated army** reads verses 19-21, also aloud and together.

You can conclude with something like this—

▶ **There's a huge battle raging between good and evil throughout the book of Revelation. It's pretty intense. But what becomes clearer and clearer and what the book progresses toward is that God is completely in control!**

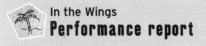

In the Wings
Performance report

What you'll need

☑ **Copies for each student of the Staging Sheet Performance Report (page 73)**

The messages to the seven churches of Asia Minor (in Revelation chapters 2-3) are almost like performance reports from Jesus. Regular report cards make your student *very familiar* with the concept of performance reports.

When your kids leave school and enter the workforce,

they'll trade a report card for a performance report—which points out not only areas in which a worker isn't performing up to par (with suggestions for improvement), but also what the worker is doing right.

So would we live differently if we got a per-formance report from Jesus at the end of every week? Lead your students in exploring perfor-mance reports that Jesus gave to seven first-century churches. Hand out the Staging Sheet **Performance Report** (page 73) for them to fill in. Ask them to work alone, to think carefully, and to be as honest as they can in what they write on their performance reports. Remind them that honesty means being aware of their shortcomings but also of their successes.

For high schoolers (Greatest hits)
Dancing through Revelation

What you'll need

☑ Copies of the Staging Sheet **Dancing through Revelation** (page 74) for each student

Revelation is fascinating but uncharted territory for many Christians and especially for teenagers. This Staging Sheet isn't intended as an in-depth Bible study, but simply as a chance to acquaint your group with the big picture in Revelation—an overview that will give your students a rough idea of the ground covered and the kind of reading they can expect in this apocalyptic book. So the majority of the group time in this part of the session goes to reading the Bible passages, with only a few basic questions to help you focus students' attention on what they're reading.

Divide your students into seven teams (see **Divide into Small Groups Creatively!** on page 75). Assign them (or let them select) a team name. Here are their choices:

- ▶ Team Death   ▶ Team Blood
- ▶ Team Famine   ▶ Team Plague
- ▶ Team Quake   ▶ Team Drought
- ▶ Team Flood

Then pass out the Staging Sheet **Dancing through Revelation** (page 74) to all students, and make sure each team sees the Revelation passage it is to read aloud and the questions on the Staging Sheet that team members are to answer.

After 15 minutes, call the group back together for a time of feedback. Work through the seven groups in order, asking each group for its opinions about the events in its passage—and, especially, if the group thinks its events have already happened, are happening now, or are yet to happen. Be careful to keep a cap on any hot debates that get started!

Then close with words to this effect—

- ▶ Having taken a look at a bizarre Bible book, maybe you can just begin to see how exciting and exhilarating Revelation can be—and also why this book is the subject of so much debate and of so many different theories.

- ▶ There may still be confusion, but one thing is totally clear—our God is in charge!

Take a Bow

Make these final points—

- ▶ Well, with Revelation we've come to the end of the Bible. Like all good movies and books, it goes out not with a whimper, but with a spectacular BANG!

- ▶ Its subject matter is powerful—heaven and hell! Good and evil! Hope and catastrophe! Resurrection! War! And the incredible imagery of apocalyptic writing make this final book a blockbuster.

- ▶ If we bring our imagination and our intelligence to bear on Revelation, it will deepen our awe and love for God and let us into one of the most wonderful "open secrets" of Christianity:

In the end, we win!

Stage Door
Bible study: what your church believes about Revelation

There are more theories about the book of Revelation than there are gobs of gum on the underside of the high school stadium bleachers—but why not at least let your students know how your church interprets the book?

Invite your pastor—or a seminary professor who happens to live nearby, or any other theo-logically qualified person—to a question-and-answer session on the book of Revelation. Your young people can get the authoritative word on how your church interprets the book, and your pastor can see firsthand that the youth group can get neck-deep in real Bible issues along with the fun and games.

Staging Sheet

Playing Cards

Mystery words

Part 1

LEADER

Mystery Word — PROPHECY

Forbidden Words

GOD
SPEAK
FUTURE
PROPHETS

Mystery Word — BOOK

Forbidden Words

PAPER
PAGES
READ
NOVEL
WRITE
PRINT

Mystery Word — CHURCH

Forbidden Words

CONGREGATION
PASTOR
WORSHIP
BUILDING
GOD
JUSUS

Mystery Word — ANGEL

Forbidden Words

WINGS
HALO
HARP
HEAVEN
CLOUDS
GUARDIAN
WHITE

Mystery words

Part 2

MS & HS

Mystery Word ——— JESUS

Forbidden Words

GOD	CROSS
ISRAEL	SAVIOR
JEW	MAN

✂ -

Mystery Word ——— EMPEROR

Forbidden Words

KING	ROMAN
RULER	EMPIRE
CAESAR	

✂ -

Mystery Word ——— CITY

Forbidden Words

TOWN	PEOPLE
CAPITAL	LIVE

✂ -

Mystery Word ——— WAR

Forbidden Words

ARMY	SOLDIER
COUNTRIES	WEAPONS
FIGHT	BATTLE
NATIONS	

✂ -

Mystery Word ——— PRISON

Forbidden Words

JAIL	CAPTIVES
CELL	BARS
PRISONERS	GUARDS
PUNISHMENT	

✂ -

A Reading in Revelation

Revelation 1:9-20

Staging Sheet

MS & HS

Characters

John

Jesus

Although this is pretty much straight from the Bible, it should be read dramatically.

JOHN: I, John, your brother and companion in the suffering and kingdom and patient endurance that are ours in Jesus, was on the island of Patmos because of the word of God and the testimony of Jesus. On the Lord's Day I was in the Spirit, and I heard behind me a loud voice like a trumpet, which said,

JESUS: Write on a scroll what you see and send it to the seven churches: to Ephesus, Smyrna, Pergamum, Thyatira, Sardis, Philadelphia and Laodicea.

JOHN: I turned around to see the voice that was speaking to me. And when I turned I saw seven golden lampstands, and among the lampstands was someone "like a son of man," dressed in a robe reaching down to his feet and with a golden sash around his chest. His head and hair were white like wool, as white as snow, and his eyes were like blazing fire. His feet were like bronze glowing in a furnace, and his voice was like the sound of rushing waters. In his right hand he held seven stars, and out of his mouth came a sharp double-edged sword. His face was like the sun shining in all its brilliance. When I saw him, I fell at his feet as though dead. Then he placed his right hand on me and said,

JESUS: Do not be afraid. I am the First and the Last. I am the Living One; I was dead, and behold I am alive for ever and ever! And I hold the keys of death and Hades. Write, therefore, what you have seen, what is now and what will take place later. The mystery of the seven stars that you saw in my right hand and of the seven golden lampstands is this: The seven stars are the angels of the seven churches, and the seven lampstands are the seven churches.

END

Revelation chapters 2 and 3 are like performance reports that Jesus gave the seven churches of Asia Minor. If Jesus were writing a weekly performance report on you, what would it say this week? Be honest about what you've done well and what you haven't done so well.

Worker _____
           your name here

Evaluator _____ Jesus _____

AREAS OF SUCCESS
List at least three things about your life that you think Jesus would be most pleased with.

AREAS FOR IMPROVEMENT
List up to three things about yourself that you're pretty sure Jesus would like you to improve.

ACTION TO BE TAKEN
List some ways you could go about making those improvements.

Dancing through Revelation

Acts 1:1-11

MS & HS

Okay, if you're not already in teams, group yourselves in 7 of 'em. Take one of these apocalyptic names for your team, then—within your own team—take turns reading your passage aloud.

- **Team Death** Revelation 4:1-5:15 • **Team Blood** Revelation 6:1-17 and 8:1-5
- **Team Famine** Revelation 8:6-9:21 and 11:15-19
- **Team Plague** Revelation 15:1-16:21 • **Team Quake** Revelation 17:1-18
- **Team Drought** Revelation 18:1-24 • **Team Flood** Revelation 21:1-22:5

As you and your team read through the passage, check the items here that you come across.

☐ trumpet	☐ sea of glass	☐ sword	☐ prostitute
☐ throne	☐ creature	☐ scale	☐ bride
☐ elder	☐ harps	☐ plague	☐ sea turned to blood
☐ sea ship	☐ beast	☐ horn	☐ sun, moon, stars
☐ famine	☐ Lamb	☐ locust	☐ thunder and lightning
☐ iMac	☐ scroll	☐ Big Mac	☐ city of gold and jewels
☐ crown	☐ altar	☐ bowl	☐ Dennis Rodman
☐ heaven	☐ white robe	☐ Babylon	☐ gold and silver
☐ abyss	☐ horse	☐ earthquake	
☐ Godzilla	☐ helicopter	☐ angel	

Now grade the passage you just read! Use the common grading scale (A-B-C-D-F) to describe your feelings about the passage.

___ **This passage was exciting to read** *(A = you wet your pants with excitement / F = you woke yourself up with your own snoring)*

___ **This passage was easy to understand** *(A = as easy to understand as Mister Rogers / F = as easy to understand as the federal budget)*

___ **This passage made me want to praise God** *(A = by the time the reading ended, you were standing on your chair, arms thrown to the ceiling, shouting, "Alleluia! Even so come, Lord Jesus!" / F = by the time the reading ended, your head was in your hands and you were muttering, "I can't believe you actually said that, God!")*

___ **This passage almost made me lose my lunch.** *(A = a big lunch, with lots of salad and tomato products / F = a small lunch, just a sandwich and milk)*

___ **It would be great to be alive when the events of this passage take/took place.** *(A = "Oh boy, I can hardly wait! Bring it all on!" / F = "Yikes! Lemme outta here!")*

So which Revelation events have already happened, which are happening even now, and which haven't yet happened? Check the box that makes most sense to you.

☐ The events of this passage took place in the past.

☐ The events of our passage are occurring right now.

☐ The events of our passage will take place in the future.

Divide into small groups creatively!

When kids get together, they often get together in cliques. It's a good idea in youth work to reshuffle these usual social orders from time to time. Small-group and pair activities like the ones in this book provide a perfect excuse for this. It's best if they're fun, too, so the students don't quite realize what you're doing. Here are the kind of tricks I use to mix the pairs or groups up and break down the usual friendship cliques.

Tallest to shortest

Ask the group to form a line with the tallest of the group standing in the front and working down gradually to the shortest of the group at the back. Then work your way down the line, assigning a number to each person. To form two teams, count off by twos: one, two, one, two, down the line. If you want to form four teams, count off by fours, and so on.

Birthdays

This method works best if you want to create three or four work groups or if there are lots of people. It isn't so good at creating more groups of fewer people,

because you tend to get too uneven a distribution of people if you place fewer months together.

To create three groups, divide the year in three. An easy division is January to April, May to August, and September to December, but you could mix the months up. Ask everyone with birthdays in the first division (say, January to April) to go stand in one corner of the room, everyone with birthdays in the second division to go stand in another corner, and everyone with birthdays in the third division to go to the third corner. There. You now have three work groups.

To make four groups, divide the months in four—January to March, April to June, July to September, and October to December.

Playing Cards

Allow the students to draw from a pile of playing cards to find their group. As the leader, you will need to make sure the right cards are in the pile before they start drawing.

To form two to four groups, you could use the four suits. Simply place the correct number of cards of each suit in a pile and allow the students to draw. The hearts form a group, the diamonds form a group, and so on.

To form a larger number of groups of four or fewer, use numbers rather than suits. For example, to form seven groups of three, you could collect aces through sevens of spades, hearts, and clubs. Put these cards in the pile and let the students draw. All the aces form one group, the deuces form another, and so on.

Draw from a Hat

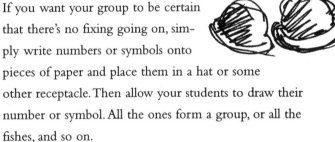

If you want your group to be certain that there's no fixing going on, simply write numbers or symbols onto pieces of paper and place them in a hat or some other receptacle. Then allow your students to draw their number or symbol. All the ones form a group, or all the fishes, and so on.

Resources from Youth Specialties

Professional Resources

Administration, Publicity, & Fundraising
  (Ideas Library)
Developing Student Leaders
Equipped to Serve: Volunteer Youth Worker
  Training Course
Help! I'm a Junior High Youth Worker!
Help! I'm a Small-Group Leader!
Help! I'm a Sunday School Teacher!
Help! I'm a Volunteer Youth Worker!
How to Expand Your Youth Ministry
How to Speak to Youth . . . and Keep Them
  Awake at the Same Time
Junior High Ministry (Updated & Expanded)
The Ministry of Nurture: A Youth Worker's
  Guide to Discipling Teenagers
Purpose-Driven Youth Ministry
So That's Why I Keep Doing This! 52
  Devotional Stories for Youth Workers
A Youth Ministry Crash Course
The Youth Worker's Handbook to Family
  Ministry

Youth Ministry Programming

Camps, Retreats, Missions, & Service Ideas
  (Ideas Library)
Compassionate Kids: Practical Ways to
  Involve Your Students in Mission
  and Service
Creative Bible Lessons from the
  Old Testament
Creative Bible Lessons in 1 & 2 Corinthians
Creative Bible Lessons in John: Encounters
  with Jesus
Creative Bible Lessons in Romans:
  Faith on Fire!
Creative Bible Lessons on the Life of Christ
Creative Junior High Programs from A to Z,
  Vol. 1 (A-M)
Creative Junior High Programs from A to Z,
  Vol. 2 (N-Z)
Creative Meetings, Bible Lessons,
  & Worship Ideas (Ideas Library)
Crowd Breakers & Mixers (Ideas Library)
Backstage Pass the Bible Leader's Guide
Drama, Skits, & Sketches (Ideas Library)
Drama, Skits, & Sketches 2 (Ideas Library)
Dramatic Pauses
Everyday Object Lessons
Games (Ideas Library)
Games 2 (Ideas Library)
Great Fundraising Ideas for Youth Groups
More Great Fundraising Ideas for
  Youth Groups

Great Retreats for Youth Groups
Holiday Ideas (Ideas Library)
Hot Illustrations for Youth Talks
More Hot Illustrations for Youth Talks
Still More Hot Illustrations for Youth Talks
Ideas Library on CD-ROM
Incredible Questionnaires for Youth Ministry
Junior High Game Nights
More Junior High Game Nights
Kickstarters: 101 Ingenious Intros to Just
  about Any Bible Lesson
Live the Life! Student Evangelism
  Training Kit
Memory Makers
The Next Level Leader's Guide
Play It! Great Games for Groups
Play It Again! More Great Games for Groups
Special Events (Ideas Library)
Spontaneous Melodramas
Student Leadership Training Manual
Super Sketches for Youth Ministry
Teaching the Bible Creatively
Videos That Teach
What Would Jesus Do? Youth Leader's Kit
Wild Truth Bible Lessons
Wild Truth Bible Lessons 2
Wild Truth Bible Lessons–Pictures of God
Worship Services for Youth Groups

Discussion Starters

Discussion & Lesson Starters (Ideas Library)
Discussion & Lesson Starters 2
  (Ideas Library)
Get `Em Talking
Keep `Em Talking!
High School TalkSheets
More High School TalkSheets
High School TalkSheets: Psalms
  and Proverbs
Junior High TalkSheets
More Junior High TalkSheets
Junior High TalkSheets: Psalms
  and Proverbs
Unfinished Sentences: 450 Tantalizing
  Statement-Starters to Get Teenagers
  Talking & Thinking
What If . . . ? 450 Thought-Provoking
  Questions to Get Teenagers Talking,
  Laughing, and Thinking
Would You Rather . . . ? 465 Provocative
  Questions to Get Teenagers Talking
Have You Ever . . . ? 450 Intriguing
  Questions Guaranteed to
  Get Teenagers Talking

Clip Art

ArtSource: Stark Raving Clip Art (print)
ArtSource: Youth Group Activities (print)
ArtSource CD-ROM: Clip Art Library
  Version 2.0

Videos

EdgeTV
The Heart of Youth Ministry: A Morning with
  Mike Yaconelli
Purpose-Driven Youth Ministry Video
  Curriculum
Understanding Your Teenager Video
  Curriculum

Student Books

Backstage Pass the Bible: A Rough Guide
  to the New Testament
Backstage Pass the Bible: A Rough Guide
  to the OldTestament
Grow For It Journal
Grow For It Journal through the Scriptures
Spiritual Challenge Journal: The Next Level
Teen Devotional Bible
What Would Jesus Do? Spiritual
  Challenge Journal
Wild Truth Journal for Junior Highers
Wild Truth Journal–Pictures of God